STRENGTHENING MY STEPS

CLAUDIA DE FAJARDO

BOGOTÁ D.C. COLOMBIA
2001

2001 © Claudia de Fajardo

Published by International Youth Mission
Tra 43 N° 15 65
Tel: 571 335 0452
mji@mji-intl.org

Printed by PANAMERICANA Formas e Impresos S.A.
Calle 65 # 95-28
Tel: 571 430 2110
Bogotá D.C.
Colombia

ISBN 958-97056-2-6

Diagramming: Camila Díaz Torres
Illustrations: Camila Díaz Torres
Revision: Luisa Del Río Saavedra

Original Title: Afirmando mis Pasos

Second English Edition January 2003   5.000 copies
First English Edition June 2001   5.000 copies
First Spanish Edition April 1999   10.000 copies
Second Spanish Edition June 2001   22.500 copies

Printed in Colombia

CONTENTS

ACKNOWLEDGEMENTS

Thank You, Lord, for all Your love and mercy that You have manifested in my life and family over the years. Thank you for giving us Your courage, tenderness, and care.

Thank You for giving me the opportunity to serve You alongside my husband César, for allowing us to see the dreams we had years ago, when we were only a few, become a reality. Thank for permitting us to make Your love and great name known, not only in Colombia, but also in the nations of the world.

I would like to thank my Pastors César and Claudia Castellanos, who have always believed in us and have given us unconditional support, allowing us to develop in our ministry. Thank you that we can always count on you, not only as pastors, but also as friends and counsellors.

You have been a great blessing to us. We love you, and thank God for your lives. We know that you are the instrument God has used to launch us into new challenges and steps of faith. These have given us many great experiences with God.

I would like to thank our team of twelve from the International Youth Mission (Misión Joven Internacional). They are excellent and such a blessing. You have been a fundamental part of the youth ministry. Each of you is a gift from God. It has been beautiful to share together through the years and watch you grow, mature, and become the great leaders that you now are.

Thank you for your faithfulness, consistency, effort, and for the unselfish giving of yourselves to others, for always being willing to give of your best.

I would like to thank the entire youth ministry for being valiant and vigorous, and for serving as the inspiration to write this material.

It is my desire that this book be useful not only in your lives, but also that it may help others in their walk with Christ. I would also like to thank Luisa Del Rio for her dedication in revising and correcting this book. Your help has been so valuable. Thank you to the design team for all your work and time invested to produce this project.

In a very special way I want to thank my beloved husband for being with me in every challenge, for playing an active role through his support, love, counsel, and patience. I know it is not easy, because behind every book there are many hours of work and dedication.

You have given me the freedom to make this dream a reality and to direct new believers in their first steps of faith. I love you, you are the man I have always dreamed of. I give thanks to God for your life because you have been not only an example to me, but you have also strengthened my heart and encouraged me to assume new challenges. Even though there is still much to conquer, we will do it together for the glory of God.

To Josué and Alejandro my two sons, I thank you for your love, patience, and tenderness and the beautiful words you have spoken to me. I know that you are both an active part of this ministry, and are increasingly allowing yourselves to be used to enlarge the work of the Lord.

Thanks to my dear mom, "Chabelita", it has been so special sharing with you. You have always been my friend and have always been there when I needed you.

Thank You, sweet Holy Spirit. I yearn for You to always be by my side, to be able to reflect Your love and presence in such a way that the world comes to know You as the real and true God that You are.

Claudia de Fajardo

INTRODUCTION

As I write these pages I think of the case of a certain teenage girl, about eighteen years old. She was enthusiastic, pleasant, and easy to get along with. One could see in her tremendous leadership and ministry potential, not only to win her family, but also to influence a great number of people.

The girl did not achieve that potential for one simple reason. She did not lay a strong enough foundation in order to continue in the path she had chosen to walk. She got involved in a relationship that was outside God's will. She became deaf to any advice, obstinate and unwilling to listen to reason. The saddest part was to watch her life take a route so different from the one that God had planned for her. The young man whom she had an ungodly relationship with it made life impossible for her, and her only way out was to end the relationship with him.

It is a shame to see how her life could have been so fulfilling had she remained faithful to God. Instead, her life was left in fear and chaos. All because she did not lay the strong foundation that would have kept her walking according to the will of God. On the other hand, I have seen people who were caught in vices and sexually promiscuous living, destroyed by the frustration in their personal and family environment. Now they are living testimonies of what God can do in a person's life. They show such overwhelming changes in their lives that one is left speechless. They now have prospering ministries. They are blessed, with an exemplary way of life and a model family, giving them great influence and also challenging those around them.

What made the difference was that some learned and practised basic Christianity. They remained with the Lord, while others, by ignorance or disobedience, did not stand firm in their decision to attain victory and receive all God had for them.

I am aware that the difference between a life of victory and one of defeat is a correct foundation in biblical principles.

These principles help you receive the abundant life that Jesus offers through His victory at the cross. For that reason I have written, "Strengthening my Steps". The purpose of this book is to give you tools to help you remain faithful in your walk with God. Here you will find a simple orientation on how to handle relationships.

You will find new alternatives to help you as a new believer, confront the habits that once enslaved you. You will be helped to conquer temptation.

We will discuss subjects such as how to draw near, through prayer, to that most marvellous being, God. You will learn how to listen to His counsel with the help of the Word as a fountain of Life and discover the church as a place of refuge. You will also learn to have a life that is balanced in order to grow in every area.

Each of the subjects is accompanied by a study that will help you deepen your knowledge in that specific area, verify what you have learned, review that lesson, or even teach it to others. What I have applied in ministry during these past ten years is found in this book. I have had the opportunity to see it produce very good results.

I have been very satisfied to see people to whom I have ministered these simple steps now serving God and teaching thousands of others. The steps worked for them. It brought them to a place where their lives are now testimony of what God can do with faithfulness to these basic and effective principles.

It is my desire that whilst reading "Strengthening my Steps" you too will gain a testimony comparable to those who have applied the teachings of this book, and live victoriously.
I want you to experience fundamental changes in your life that will cause you to become a challenge to others and also a channel of blessing through which God can freely flow.

Claudia de Fajardo

PROLOGUE

How exciting life is once we have accepted Jesus as our Lord!

I have been an evangelist for many years and I have seen multitudes of people touched by the power of God. I have seen tremendous healings, deliverances, and great miracles wrought by the power of God.

To me the most important moment is that in which people make the decision to follow Christ with all of their heart. I have seen them run to the altar with eyes full of tears, expressing their desire to follow Christ and never leave Him.

It is at this moment of turning to God that one's life truly feels complete. This personal encounter with Jesus Christ produces many changes in us. It is a profound transformation inside our being, and as a result many questions arise in our lives that now need answers.

We have entered into a new life with God, and we begin to question ourselves about how we have lived and acted in the past. We urgently need answers through the light of the Word of God to expel the ignorance concerning our new walk with the Lord.

It is after choosing Christ that we get tested. The enemy tries to turn us back to the old way without God.

In times of testing, even our family and friends can become instruments used by the enemy. Pressure, criticism, and misunderstanding come, because of the decisions we have made.

Many new believers turn back from their walk with God because they have not been firmly established in their knowledge of the Word and above all, they do not know the practical steps to live a victorious Christian life.

The decision for Christ is just the beginning, from that point begins a long process transforming us into the image an likeness of God. We need answers to the questions asked by new believers. We must help them in their daily walk with Jesus. If we do not help, then that exciting moment of receiving Jesus will become simply a story, a memory that has no effect on their lives.

We give thanks to God because this book by Claudia de Fajardo will fill the emptiness and answer the questions of those just starting their Christian life. "Strengthening my Steps" marks out the course for every person who has made the decision to follow Jesus.

STRENGTHENING MY STEPS is a book that will instruct you in your walk with Christ. How to live to please Him and how to endure the temptations, trials, and struggles that come when we begin to walk with Him. But above all it will give you biblical and practical solutions to be applied in every situation you face each day as a Christian.

Through this book, you will develop a deep intimate relationship with Christ. You will come to know Him and experience more of His presence. This will create in you the desire to live in holiness and get rid of the many things that separated you from God in the past.

As a result of communion with God and holiness you will begin to develop a life of authority. This book will teach you how to use that influence in a society that is in desperate need of examples of true Christians.

It is the Lord's desire to mould you into a true Christian through this book. It has pleased God to bless Claudia's ministry not only because she writes about something she knows in theory, but because she has practised that theory as an instrument of God to shape many lives. This book has gathered her vast experience and the principles she has taught multitudes.

May I congratulate you on your decision to accept Christ as the Lord of your life and to consecrate your life to Him- but don't stop there! As you study this book let the conviction of a new life and testimony take root in you, so that you may be blessed, and also bless many other people.

Allow God to make you an instrument in His hands. We give thanks to God for giving His servant Claudia the revelation to prepare such a marvellous work, which if applied to our daily lives, will produce eternal results.

Dr. Omar Cabrera
Iglesia Visión del Futuro
Buenos Aires, Argentina

HOW TO OVERCOME THE WORLD

Many people, after returning from an Encounter weekend, desire to radically follow the Lord in every area of their life. They want nothing from the world. Nevertheless, because they do not know how to handle various situations, they allow themselves to be conquered by circumstances.

People return very motivated. They have abandoned drugs, bad influences, and everything that had been enslaving them.However, they give in to temptation soon after because they do not know how to deal with it.

One young man had just returned from an Encounter and being a new student at university, wanted to be accepted by his classmates. He did not want to be considered a fanatic. On one occasion he accompanied them to a pub. His only intention was to drink lemonade, but he ended up drinking beer, taking drugs, and once again became enslaved by Satan.

Time passed, and he left university and his home. He began living a life of misery, selling his clothes for drugs, and getting into fights. His arms were scarred from stab wounds and his life marked by unhappiness.

I. WHAT IS THE WORLD ?

A. The World

The world represents everything that displeases God, opposes His teaching, and is under Satan's dominion.
(I John 5:19)

Many philosophies, ideas, and doctrines distort or degrade Christ and His sacrifice on the cross of Calvary. These offer a salvation not found in the Word of God, and are all manifestations of the world.

The Apostle John points out three aspects that mark the love of this world: the desires of the flesh, the desires of the eyes, and the pride of life.

> «Do not love the world or the things in the world. If anyone loves the world, the love of the Father is not in him. For all that is in the world - the lust of the flesh, the lust of the eyes, and the pride of life - is not of the Father but is of the world. And the world is passing away, and the lust of it; but he who does the will of God abides forever.»
>
> **I John 2:15-17**

B. Lust of the flesh

These are those desires that are in us by nature and impel us to do the wrong thing. They incite us, even from childhood, to yield to what the flesh desires. They can be described as the satisfaction, passion, or enjoyment that is felt by doing wrong things. In doing these things, we give room to sin in our lives.

Galatians 5:17 says:

"For the flesh lusts against the Spirit, and the Spirit against the flesh; and these are contrary to one another, so that you do not do the things that you wish."

This shows the conflict found in every Christian life. The flesh wants one thing, while the spirit wants another. That is why it is important to nourish our spiritual man.

Gal 5:19-21 gives us a long list of the sins of the flesh. These include sexual sins, sins involving pagan religions such as witchcraft or idolatry and other sins relating to temperament and character.

The fruit of the Spirit is everything that is opposite to the flesh.
In relation to God: love, joy, and peace.
In relation to others: patience, kindness, and goodness.
In relation to ourselves: faith, kindness, and self-control.

Our goal should be that our spirit wins the battle against the flesh.
Dr. Billy Graham gives us this illustration:

"Every Saturday afternoon a fisherman would walk down into the village. He would always take his two dogs with him. One was white and the other black. He had taught them to fight at his command. Every week, people would gather in the town square to place bets and watch the dogs fight.

One Saturday the black dog would win, another Saturday the white dog would win, but the fisherman would always win! His friends began to ask him how he did it. He said, "I let one dog go hungry while I feed the other one. The one I feed always wins because he feels stronger."

If we want to conquer the desires of the flesh, we have to pay special attention to our spirit. We must feed it and care for it in such a way that in the face of temptation, the spirit prevails.

C. Lust of the Eye

The eyes can be a fountain of life, purity, and inspiration, or they can be an instrument of evil, perversion, and bad desires. Dr. W.E. Vine describes them as being, *"the principal avenue to temptation."* "The desires of the eyes" can be described as perversions, bad intentions, and selfish delights that include not only the sight, but also the mind and imagination.

The Bible teaches in 2 Peter 2:14

> *"having eyes full of adultery and that cannot cease from sin,..."*

And in Matthew 5:27-29:

> You have heard that it was said to those of old, 'You shall not commit adultery'. But I say to you that whoever looks at a woman to lust for her has already committed adultery with her in his heart.

The word "look" refers to the desires of the eyes, a look laden with lust, which wakens impure images and desires in our minds. Someone once said, "The first look isn't sinful, but the second one is." This second look aims to satisfy the mind's own desires.

Beacon's Commentary says that this type of lust is "the tendency to be captivated by the exterior appearance of things without looking into its real worth."

The lust of the eyes includes not only sight, but also the mind and imagination. They seek to satisfy themselves through pornography or unedifying books, magazines, or movies.

They create an addiction that can only be quenched by giving in to the pleasures of the flesh.

Generally, these desires are fed by thoughts convincing us that sin is something pleasant, pleasurable, and desirable. We justify the sinful thought as being acceptable, as something harmless and insignificant. And since we haven't actually done anything, we are convinced it is not sin. What's more, it keeps us from seeing the consequences that our behavior may bring to our own lives and to those that we love.

A common example is when the mind delights itself with memories of past sexual experiences, drunkenness, parties, or gambling. The enemy shows you the fun you experienced, the pleasures you felt, and how wonderful it would be to experience them again. These memories are accompanied by thoughts like, "there's nothing wrong with that," or, "everyone is doing it," or, "I can't become a fanatic."

The mind does not concentrate on the consequences that will come sooner or later, but on the desire and pleasures it wants to feel again.

As we can see, the influence the lust of the eye has on us is acute. They manipulate our mind and cause us to forget what Christ did for us. That is why it is good to follow the Apostle Paul's counsel, when he exhorts us to walk in the Spirit and to not satisfy the desires of the flesh.

D. Pride of life

This refers to the belief that the reason for life is found in the worldly appearance and worth of things, and not in how God actually values them.
Pride is the illusion that leads people into superficiality, inflates their egos, and makes them believe that their worth is based on position, money and friends.

These "vanities" turn into strongholds for people who open the door to them. Vanities lead them to believe that their own ability has given them positions of importance with their peers. For this reason, some people climb over others in life, violating biblical principles and the will of God. Behind their appearances they hide their insecurity.

An example of this is when you spend more than you earn and live in debt even though it steals your peace.
You don't change because you want to pretend that you are rich.
You buy designer clothes, expensive mobile phone, or hang out at the most popular places. You have been led to think these things win people's respect.

God wants us to be prosperous. When we love Him, He lifts us to a better position. God, not His blessings, gives us our value. If we seek Him first, the rest will be added to us. God, not money, will give us respect and authority.

II. HOW THE WORLD AFFECTS ME

The young person's world is not a secret to anyone. It is one that offers parties, vices, sinful passions, and a worthless and empty life.

The media (radio, press, and television) along with society push us towards this type of lifestyle. They trick us into believing that to have fun you must become part of their activities.
If we refuse, we are labelled as boring and bitter people. These words, boring and bitter are the most commonly used words by non-Christians to pressure the believer into doing what they want or say.

The world may affect me when I give into its ways. It affects me when I take part in its dirty jokes and perverted comments or accept its invitation to drink and party. It affects me when these activities stop being fun and become addictive, when I end up caught in circumstances that I want to be free from, but cannot.

For example, an ungodly relationship ends in frustration and deception; an excess of alcohol produces sicknesses such as cirrhosis and venereal diseases are a result of a degenerate and promiscuous life.

The life the world offers us is a mirror that makes us believe that it is true and fulfilling. However, it doesn't let us see the deception and true consequences of its ways.

Jesus does not want to remove us from the world. He wants us to shine and be a light wherever we are. He said:

> I do not pray that You should take them out of the world, but that You should keep them from the evil one.
> **John 17:15**

III. HOW TO FACE THE WORLD NOW THAT I AM CHRISTIAN

A. Not participating in what the world has to offer

Ephesians 5:11 says:

«And have no fellowship with the unfruitful works of darkness, but rather expose them.»

Right from the start you need to learn how to be radical in dealing with sin. Don't ever cloud the real issues. For example, if they offer you a drink, don't lie by saying, "No thank you, I'm on medication and drinking could be harmful." That is not true. You are not on medication. It is rather a matter of faith, but you are too embarrased to tell the truth.

B. Be radical in your stand as a Christian

Job 22:28 says

«You will also declare a thing, And it will be established for you; So light will shine on your ways»

Decide beforehand what things you are not going to yield to. For example, decide not to go to parties with non-believers or social events where drinking and other vices are predominant.

By deciding ahead of time you will avoid facing temptation and prevent yourself from falling into sin. The main thing is to decide, "No matter what happens, I will not leave the path that I have chosen." This is determination.
When I do my part God does His.
He brings His light to reveal what we should say or do.

C. Avoid spending too much time with unbelievers

They will constantly encourage you to do wrong, inciting you to turn back.

D. Look for friends that share the same purpose and goals

Spend time with those people who challenge you and strengthen your relationship with God.

E. Strengthen your relationship with God

Spend time with Him daily in prayer and live in such a way that you will not leave His side. When you are facing situations that you are uncertain and doubtful about, it will help to ask yourself, "What would Jesus do if He were in my place?

«I will no longer talk much with you, for the ruler of this world is coming, and he has nothing in Me.»
John 14:30

EXERCISE
HOW TO OVERCOME THE WORLD

1. The word "world" does not refer to the literal world we live in, but rather it refers to whatever opposes God. According to **1 John 5:19**, who rules this world?

_____

_____

2. According to **1 John 2:16**, what are the specific things that show the love of this world?

a. _____

b. _____

c. _____

3. **1 John 2:15** says this concerning the world (tick the right answer):

a. We should hide from it

b. We should love and care for it

c. We should not love it

d. We should accept it and live by it

4. What are the desires of the flesh?

_____

_____

_____

_____

5. In every Christian, a battle rages between the flesh and the spirit. What should we do if we want to conquer the desires of the flesh?

_____

_____

6. The lust of the eye include not only sight, but also the mind and imagination. How do these desires try to satisfy themselves?

_____

_____

7. What is most valuable for those who live out of pride?

_____

_____

8. Jesus does not want us to be influenced by the world. On the contrary, we are to shine and be a light wherever we are. In **John 17:15**, what did Jesus ask of the Father concerning His disciples?

    a. That they would stay indoors so as to not be tempted
    b. That they would sin, but only a very little bit
    c. That they would die so they would not sin
    d. That He would not take them out of the world but rather guard them from evil

REMEMBER,
WE STILL LIVE IN THIS WORLD, SO IT IS NECESSARY
TO DETERMINE WHAT THINGS WE WILL NOT YIELD TO.

9. What things in this world will I not give into?

    a. _____

    b. _____

10. From the very start, we have to be radical when it comes to sin, honestly showing who we now are. According to **Ephesians 5:11:**

    a. What should I not do?

    _____

    b. What should I do?

_____

11. From now on, it is best that your friends be (tick the right answer):

    a. Those who challenge you and strengthen your relationship with God
    b. Those who are caught in the world's deceit suffering the
       consequences
    c. Those who continually pressure you to turn back

REMEMBER,
IN DOUBTFUL OR UNCERTAIN
SITUATIONS ASK YOURSELF,
WHAT WOULD JESUS DO IF HE WERE IN MY PLACE?

HOW TO TALK WITH GOD

Everyone that yearns to live in victory needs to learn to depend on God through daily prayer. Prayer is the opportunity God has given us to talk to Him - the greatest of all beings, the almighty, to Whom nothing is impossible. A consistent prayer life gives us the power to overcome all things.

Prayer is dynamite. Tremendous things can come into the lives of those who pray daily. That is why we should make it a lifestyle. It should be something that forms part of our way of living, a habit just like eating, sleeping, or brushing your teeth.

Jesus made a habit out of prayer. He would find a place where He could be alone with the Father. Mark 1:35 says:

> "Now in the morning, having risen up a long while before daylight, He went out and departed into a solitary place, and there He prayed."

I. THE IMPORTANCE OF PRAYER

As believers in Christ, we should follow in the footsteps of our Teacher. This means setting aside time to be alone with God, preferably in the morning. We can then hear His direction, receive His protection and support in the different situations that we will face throughout the rest of the day.

To pray effectively, find the most convenient time for you, regardless of whether it is during the day or at night. Pray by yourself, so that you can have intimacy with God, freely pouring out your heart without any inhibitions. Praying in church or with other Christians is enjoyable when you begin your life with God. But praying by yourself has advantages and will teach you not to depend on praying with other people.

The Lord teaches us how to pray in Matthew 6:6

> "But you, when you pray, go into your room, and when you have shut your door, pray to your Father who is in the secret place: and your Father who sees in secret will reward you openly."

The advantage of praying in private is that since no one else is listening, we can tell God everything we feel, want, or are worried about. We can go to Him with our faults and virtues because He knows us for who we are. He knows our thoughts and intentions even before we tell Him. God enjoys listening to us and jealously longs for us. His desire is to help and direct us through prayer and His Word.

Have a certain time and place for a "daily appointment" with God to develop your prayer habit. If for some reason you do not have your devotional, don't fall into legalism or guilt. Rather, learn your lesson and try even harder to meet with the Lord next time. He never misses an appointment, and without a doubt He will be waiting for you to give you His love, blessing and to take away your burdens.

In Matthew 11:28 God expresses His desire to help us:

> "Come to Me, all you who labour and
> are heavy laden, and I will give you rest."

The invitation is for those who "labour" that is, those who are in tribulation, in affliction, physically or emotional wounded. You can give Him every burden that you have been enduring, and suffering. God knows your situation, and as Isaiah 63:9 says, "In all their affliction He was afflicted."

He can relate to with your pain, which is why He says to us: "Come with all that you have, family problems, emotional needs, come with your studies, or with your work, and I will give you rest."

Prayer is pouring out your heart, which implies more than mechanically repeating phrases while your mind dwells on other things. Praying is talking with understanding, conscious that we are talking with an intelligent being. Even though we do not see Him, His presence is with every person who decides to seek Him with their whole heart.

The Lord says:

"...And the one that comes to me I will by no means cast out." **John 6:37**

If we seek Him He will be there and will receive us, not ignore us. That is the reason we should not pray lip-service prayers, but rather heart-prayers; prayers that we can remember so that we recognise the answer when it comes.

II. HOW TO BE EFFECTIVE IN PRAYER

a. Start your prayer time realising you are in the presence of God.

Hebrews 11:6 **says :**

"But without faith it is impossible to please Him, for he who comes to God must believe that He is, and that He is a rewarder of those who diligently seek Him."

b. Then confess to God whatever sins you have committed with words, thoughts, or actions, so that your prayers will not be hindered.

Psalm 66:18 **affirms:**

"If I regard iniquity in my heart, The Lord will not hear."

c. Spend time presenting your specific needs. Jesus included them in the Lord's Prayer when He said:

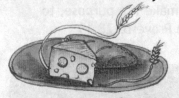

> "Give us this day our daily bread."
> **Matthew 6:11**

Therefore, take advantage of the opportunity to make your requests in the name of Jesus. John 16:24 teaches us:

> " Until now you have asked nothing in my name. Ask, and you will receive, that your joy may be full."

d. Determine to give God the best of your time, not just what is left over. Be fully convinced that you are making the best investment of your life. Nothing opens up bigger doors of opportunities than your relationship with God. And it will also guard you from temptation.
Matthew 26:41 warns:

> "Watch and pray, lest you enter into temptation. The spirit indeed is willing, but the flesh is weak."

As you become more familiar with talking to God, you will be able to include other people in your prayers, which can accomplish great things on their behalf. Let God lead you to pray for certain answers,and believe you will see them. End your devotional time by thanking God for having received His blessings and for all He is doing in your life.

You need to realise that God is by your side throughout the day, and you can talk to Him every time you need to. He delights in you doing so. You will feel that He is a part of your life and it will be a way to show Him your love.

e. Before going to sleep examine your life, ask the Lord what things (thoughts, attitudes, words, or actions) have displeased Him. Then, confess those things and make it a purpose, to leave them behind. The Word says in Proverbs 28:13

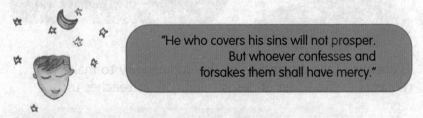

"He who covers his sins will not prosper. But whoever confesses and forsakes them shall have mercy."

Then, ask the Holy Spirit for strength to continue and the ability to live according to His will. End by thanking Him for the victory.

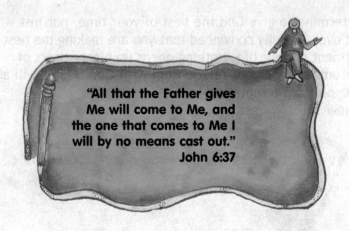

"All that the Father gives Me will come to Me, and the one that comes to Me I will by no means cast out."
John 6:37

EXERCISE
HOW TO TALK WITH GOD

1. Whoever yearns to have a victorious life needs to learn to depend on God (Tick the right answer):

> a. On Sundays, covering the whole coming week
> b. On the day of your cell group
> c. Daily
> d. Whenever you have problems

2. Tick the correct answer
   Prayer is:

> a. An obligation
> b. A requirement
> c. An opportunity

> SINCE GOD IS AN ALMIGHTY GOD,
> NOTHING EMPOWERS US MORE THEN A LIFE
> OF CONSTANT COMMUNICATION WITH HIM.

3. Since prayer accomplishes tremendous things, what should it be to us?

> a. A _____ of _____
> b. Part of _____ of _____
> c. And of our_____

4. Why is it better to talk to God by yourself than with people present?

_____
_____
_____

5. According to **Matthew 6:6**

   a. When we pray we should:

   _____

   b. When I pray in secret, God....

   _____

> REMEMBER
> GOD DELIGHTS IN HEARING YOU. HE JEALOUSLY
> DESIRES IT AND LONGS TO HELP YOU! SET
> ASIDE TIME FOR YOUR APPOINTMENT WITH HIM.

6. If you were not able to have your devotions (your time alone with God) you should:

   a. Go around all day with a guilt complex
   b. Never pray again because God is angry
   c. Leave things that way— it is not that important
   d. Learn your lesson and ensure you don't miss the next
       appointment with Him

7. According to **Matthew 11:28**, what should we do when we are burdened or when we are physically or emotionally afflicted?

   _____

8. What should we do to have a good time in prayer?

   _____
   _____
   _____
   _____

9. According to **John 6:37**, if we go to the Lord....

   _____

10. Taking into account that our prayer should not be formal but rather from the heart, what will our prayers be like according to:

    a. Hebrews 11:6 _____

_____

    b. Psalm 66:18 _____

_____

    c. John 16:24 _____

_____

GOD IS WITH YOU DURING THE DAY.
TALK TO HIM EVERY TIME YOU NEED TO.
IN ALL YOUR ACTIVITIES AND ALSO BEFORE
GOING TO BED, ASK HIM TO SEARCH YOU AND
HELP YOU MAINTAIN YOUR RELATIONSHIP WITH HIM.

SOCIAL LIFE

We are social beings by nature. We need others in order to be fulfilled. Genesis 2:18 says, "It is not good that man should be alone."

Christianity is not a synonym for isolation. As Christians we need to learn how to manage our relationships within our social circle without letting them have a negative effect on us. On the contrary, we need to have a positive influence on them.

Jeremiah 15:19 teaches us, "Let them return to you, but you must not return to them."

I. OUR FIRST CHALLENGE: THE PEOPLE THAT SURROUND US

After receiving Christ the first issue that we face is dealing with our family, lifelong friends, fellow students or workers and acquaintances.

All of these people confront us with:
«Is it true you have become a Christian? Don't tell me you don't drink anymore! Don't believe everything they tell you over there! Is it true they don't allow you to have boyfriends? You've let them brainwash you!
We have all found ourselves faced with questions and statements like these. So how do we act in front of this type of people?

II. HOW TO BEHAVE IN FRONT OF NON-BELIEVERS

A. Act calmly and with conviction

It will not be hard to face questions that are intentionally antagonistic if you are fully convinced that you have made the right decision and chosen what is the right lifestyle. This knowledge will give you security and conviction. When the opponents of Jesus cunningly tried to trick Him with questions, he left them speechless with His answers. You will do the same because He will be the One talking through you.
For example, Jesus was asked, "Is it lawful for us to pay taxes to Caesar or not?" But He perceived their craftiness, and said

to them, "Why do you test Me? Show Me a denarius. Whose image and inscription does it have?" They answered and said, "Caesar's" And He said to them, "Render therefore to Caesar the things that are Caesar's, and to God the things that are God's." But they could not catch Him in His words in the presence of the people, and they marvelled at His answer and kept silent." (Luke 20:22-26).

That same Jesus is by your side, so you do not need to be intimidated. His Word says:

> "Whoever believes on Him will not be put to shame."
> **Romans 10:11**

Act naturally, and calmly respond saying, "Now I am truly enjoying life, and you guys don't know what you are missing!"
If they respond with irony and criticism, don't get upset, keep calm and tell them you are not going to give up on what you now believe just to make them happy.

Being radical means that people will try to pressure you to give into their desires. But when they see your firm stand, they will respect you to the point that when they have problems, you will be the person they turn to!

Remember! Nothing makes the kingdom of darkness happier than an angry or out-of-control Christian. The adversary enjoys this, because when you get angry you lose your authority with people, which gives your opponents reason to ridicule you. The smartest thing to do is put Peter's advice into practice:

> "But sanctify the Lord God in your hearts, and always be ready to give a defence to everyone that asks you a reason for the hope that is in you, with meekness and fear."
> **1 Peter 3:15**

B. Worry about pleasing God and not man

Satan will try to make you afraid of what others will say and how they may ridicule you. He may tell you that to fail in the eyes of men or to lose acceptance from a group of people is the worst thing that could happen. Many allow the enemy to deceive them in this and deny Jesus in order to be accepted by their friends.

If you are ashamed of God, it is because you do not love Him enough and prefer being approved by man rather than by God. Consequently you will end up without God's approval and ultimately without man's.

King Saul chose to please men instead of God, which caused God to reject him as King. It also caused Saul to lose his influence over people (1Samuel 15:24). God then raised up a man, David, who loved Him above everything and everyone else. He risked his life to fight against the giant Goliath and won honour for the name of God. This deed lifted him up, not only before God, but also before all of Israel.
(1Samuel 17:45-46 and 18:6-7)

The key for us is to remember Christ's sacrifice at Calvary and decide to show the Lord that it was not in vain. We should be Christians of conviction, not of convenience.

Don't act spiritual in church and then outside act as if you did not know Christ. Treat the Lord as you would someone you deeply love, defending Him when others are hurting or mistreating Him. Recognise He is worthy to be honoured and pleased, even if you lose the respect of others by doing it.

Karl Marx's father changed his convictions when he went from Germany to England. In England it was "convenient" for him to lay aside the Jewish convictions he had practiced all his life. His son lost all faith in God after seeing the hypocrisy of his father. This led him to declare that "religion is the opium of the people".

> "But whoever denies Me before men, him I will also deny before my Father who is in heaven."
> **Matthew 10:33**

Having this truth in mind you need to renounce being a secret disciple of Jesus, and confess Him before man so that He will confess you before the Father. You have no reason to feel ashamed when asked malicious questions or when you are made fun of. Don't give in to their demands to prove you are not fanatical.

C. Understand your new position in Christ

As believers we are to be lights shining on no matter who we meet. The Bible says:

> "You are the light of the world." **Matthew 5:14**

Being a light is living as Christ would live if He were in our place. We have to make a difference in the world. It seems crazy to those accustomed to their old way of life, but they cannot understand because they are carnal and unspiritual.

> "But the natural man does not receive the things of the Spirit of God, for they are foolishness to him: nor can he know them, because they are spiritually discerned."
> **1 Corinthians 2:14**

This is why others do not understand the path you have chosen, but you need to be convinced that you have made the right choice. Time will prove you right and you will be able to say:

> "Now to him who is able to do exceeding abundantly above all that we ask or think, according to the power that works in us"
> **Ephesians 3:20**

Since you have God on your side, all who attack you calling you fanatical, crazy, or religious, will eventually see that your God is real and that your decision was wise and true.

Being a "light" might make some people feel uncomfortable as your new lifestyle will highlight their bad habits and customs. The Bible teaches this:

> "For everyone practising evil hates the light and does not come into the light, lest his deeds should be exposed."
> **John 3:20**

For this reason they will try to deny Christianity and what it represents, and get you to fall back into your old way of life, which produced nothing good.
The Word advices us:

> " My son, if sinners entice you, do not consent...
> My son, do not walk in the way with them,
> Keep your foot from their path."
> **Proverbs. 1:10,15**

The writer of this proverb teaches us to separate ourselves from our past life. To keep away from people that had a bad influence on us and led us into sin, deceiving us by telling us that it is the right thing to do.

We need to understand that the world does not want the best for us, but for us to drown in a life of slavery and emptiness. That is why we need to be wise and choose true friendships that will help us become better people.

I heard of a situation where a young lady returned from an Encounter weekend on fire for Christ, but began spending a lot of time with her lifelong boyfriend. The boyfriend pressured her to conform to the old sinful activities they used to do.

One day, when they were together her boyfriend invited her to a night club, but the she refused. The friend responded by saying, "You can't say no to a friend." Instead of standing firm as a light and making a difference, she gave into to her friend's pressure and went with him. Returning for the nightclub, she felt the weight of conviction come upon her which comes when we fail the Lord and fall back into old vices. At least she then sought help from a mature Christian instead of staying in guilt and sin. She learnt her lesson and was restored before God and man.

A. Form a new group of friends

Believers who have no Christian friends will find it difficult to continue strongly. You must find a new group of friends who share your new way of life.

To do this you must apply Proverbs 18:24

> "A man who has friends must himself be friendly..."

Talking with people in the church, knowing how to listen and answer them courteously will help you make friends and learn to love and value them.

The best way to make new friends is by faithfully going to a cell group, net meetings, and Sunday services. Always have an open and friendly attitude that instills confidence in those to whom you talk. Don't use abrupt responses in conversation such as "Yes", "No" and "Fine". These phrases leave the people you are talking to without a subject of conversation and without the desire to talk to you again.

It is important that you become friends with the most committed people in the church. They will challenge your life by keeping you from becoming mediocre, or from a self righteous attitude because you no longer practice the shameful sins of the past.

Proverbs 13:20 **advises:**

> "He who walks with wise men will be wise, but the companion of fools will be destroyed."

It is not wise to spend time with the wrong type of people, those who have a negative influence over your life and tempt you to turn away from God. They will cause you to backslide and give up on a Christian life. Their constant pressure may overwhelm you, and cause you to sin and eventually fall.

There is a popular saying which states, "Tell me who you walk with, and I will tell you who you are." People you feel the most comfortable with and share most of your time with are the biggest reflection of who you really are.

III. TAKE THE CHALLENGE TO WIN YOUR FRIENDS

A. Show the positive things that God has done in you

Do it! Be a good testimony to your family, friends, and acquaintances. Paul advises:

> "You, therefore, who teach another, do you not teach yourself? You who preach that a man should not steal, do you steal?... You who make your boast in the law, do you dishonour God through breaking the law? For "The name of God is blasphemed among the Gentiles because of you." as it is written."
>
> **Romans 2:21, 23-24**

Nothing is more harmful in winning others than to say one thing and do another. That is why you need to be consistent wherever you are.
If you do fail, have an attitude of humility, restore the damage done and allow your life to reflect the love of God.

B. Witness to others with wisdom

a. Avoid having a condemning attitude, showing off as being super-spiritual, and looking at others as vile sinners.

b. Don't use terms around them such as, "Hallelujah," and "Praise God." These sound good in church, but for someone who does not know God this can be strange.

c. Do not mention about learning to speak in tongues or about deliverance to non-Christians. This will be very hard for them to understand or accept.

d. Do not force your beliefs and doctrines on anyone. The Holy Spirit is the One who convincts people of their sin, not you.

e. Avoid pointless discussions and meaningless arguments that instead of drawing people closer to God, actually drive them farther away.

C. Include your friends in your prayers

Prayer has the power to change everything. That is why you should take advantage of it and win your friends to the Lord. It is much better to have your friends on your side than against you.

There was a young man who was accustomed to living an unruly life. When he came back from an Encounter he inmediately demonstrated a change of lifestyle. This changed his previously bad reputation. He was no longer deeply dissatisfied. He had a peace, so unlike the fleeting happiness that many sins give. At the same time, he included his three best friends in his daily prayers and consequently won them for the Lord. Now they all serve God together.

Always believe what James 5:16 says: "The effective, fervent prayer of a righteous man avails much." Persevere! That is the only way you will win your friends for Jesus.

Apply these three things and renew your mind. Remember that you have the answer for the world's need. Therefore, if at first they reject you, don't understand you, or don't accept you, persevere in thinking right and acting correctly. This will make you strong in faith and godly purpose.

In time they will search for what you have, and one day you will see them enjoying the blessings that come from living in Christ.

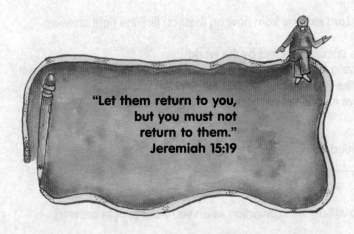

"Let them return to you, but you must not return to them."
Jeremiah 15:19

EXERCISE
SOCIAL LIFE

1. The Lord expects from now on that you (tick the right answer):

a. Live uncontaminated by the world
b. Have a lot of friends, regardless of whether they serve God or not
c. Be like your "friends" so that they still like you
d. Have friends but not know how to choose them

2. Around non-believers I should act with _____ and
_____ as _____ did.

3. You will act with conviction when you (tick the right answer):

    a. Think being a Christian is good but not great
    b. Sometimes believe and sometimes don't
    c. Are fully convinced of having made the right decision
    d. Go to church because you are told to

REMEMBER,
IF YOU ARE NOT CONVINCED OF WHAT YOU BELIEVE
YOU WILL NOT BE ABLE TO CONVINCE OTHERS!

4. Jesus gave us the example of acting with calm conviction in
Luke 20:22-26. After reading it, we can draw the following conclusions:

a. Were they asking because they really wanted to know the answer or
rather to tempt Him?

_____

_____

b. What did Jesus do when He discovered their intentions?

    a. He got upset
    b. He left and did not let them speak
    c. He answered them without arguing-He knew He was right

**AS WITH JESUS, PEOPLE WILL ASK YOU QUESTIONS INTENDING
TO DISCOURAGE YOU.
DON'T FALL INTO THEIR TRAP!**

5. Write out **Romans 10:11**

_____

_____

6. Complete in first person **I Peter 3:15**

_____

_____

_____

_____

_____

7. How did David show God he loved Him? **I Samuel 15:24-30**

_____

_____

8. According to **Mathew 10:33** if I deny Jesus before man what will He do?

_____

_____

9. What is our new position in Christ according to **Matthew 5 :14?**

_____

YOU HAVE THE POWER OF GOD AND THAT POWER WILL
WORK MIRACLES IN YOUR LIFE SO THOSE WHO USED TO
ATTACK YOU WILL EVENTUALLY ACCEPT THAT YOUR
GOD IS REAL AND THAT YOUR DECISION WAS RIGHT!

10. What is King Solomon's advice in **Proverbs 1:10,15**?

_____

_____

_____

11. Having friends is an indispensable part of your Christian life. How can
you make friends according to **Proverbs 18:24**?

_____

_____

12. **Proverbs 13:20** says that if you want to be wise you must:

_____

_____

THE WORD
- THE FOUNTAIN
OF LIFE

On a certain occasion a young man purchased a liner ticker to take an extensive trip. It was a dream come true.

During his trip he ate almost nothing because he had spent all of his money on the ticket. He did not think he could afford to pay a restaurant bill on the ship. On the last day of the journey, feeling he could no longer endure the hunger, he headed to the restaurant saying to himself, "Even if I have to pay the bill by washing dishes, I must have a proper meal."

He was so surprised when he asked the waiter for the bill and the waiter said, "No sir, you do not own anything, your ticket covers all the meals during the voyage."

Often we are the same. We have the fountain of provision and blessings in our hands - the Word of God. But though we have this fountain of life with its promises, we do exactly as the young man in the story. We live without enjoying all of the good things God has for us, ignoring the Word, and missing His promises and blessings.

We need to love the Word and follow its instructions, just as a captain of a ship follows his compass. Doing this we will learn how to act with wisdom and get the most we can out of the Bible for our lives. The Bible is the greatest of all treasures. It has the answers to all our needs, tells us how to manage our finances, and how to deal with problems, family, and emotions. Joshua 1:8 says:

> "This Book of the Law shall not depart from your mouth, but you shall meditate in it day and night, that you may observe to do according to all that is written in it. For then you will make your way prosperous, and then you will have good success."

God has given us His Word for a purpose. It is to be the daily guide by wich we walk, and it is the measure of all our decisions and circumstances.
The Psalmist says in Psalm 119:105:

> "Your word is a lamp to my feet and a light to my path"

God inspired different men in diverse times and cultures to write the Word, the Bible, so we could know Him and receive His promises. But how are we to understand, make use of and practice the Word to make our ways prosperous and right?

I. HOW TO APPROACH THE WORD

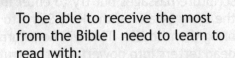

To be able to receive the most from the Bible I need to learn to read with:

A. The right attitude

That is to say, with an expectation to receive the counsel of the wisest Being in the universe. We must realize that the Bible is the means through which God speaks to His beloved, the church. We need to read it with the same interest and focus that a person in love would read a letter from his girlfriend - reading it over and over again, to catch all that it is conveying.

You need to ask God to open up your understanding, just as Jesus did for His disciples. Luke 24:45 says, "And He opened their understanding, that they might comprehend the Scriptures." This is fundamental to the working of the Word in your life. When your understanding is opened, the Word becomes light, and you will be able to understand things in a way that will actually impact your life.

When the Word is able to impact your heart it becomes your fountain of life. It establishes principles that guide you in your daily life. It changes the way you think and live.

B. Meditate in it

The best way to meditate on the Word is by asking yourself questions about the passage you are reading. You can ask yourself, "What can this teach me?", "How can I apply what I have read?" or, "With what person do I identify most?," or, "What is God trying to tell me here?," and so on.

It will also help if you not only read scripture passages but try to enter in to the story by asking the Holy Spirit to bring them to life. This will help turn dead letters into powerful active truth, influencing you to pray with more strength and commitment.

Joshua 1:8 says, "This Book of the Law shall not depart from your mouth" the invitation to meditate on the book of the law, (the Word of God), is one we should accept all day and night not just for a few moments now and again. The Word helps, leads, and strengthens us in all of our daily activities. The Lord motivates us in this passage to continually confess the Word, saying, "You shall meditate in it day and night..."

C. Obedience

The purpose of meditating on the Word is expressed in Joshua 1:8 when it reads, "But you shall meditate in it day and night, that you may observe to do according to all that is written it. For then you will make your way prosperous, and then you will have good success."

The object is to learn obedience and have a sensitive heart to do all that God has indicated. The idea is not just to receive information but that the Word of God penetrate our hearts, impact us, and change our way of living.

James explains it like this:

> "But be doers of the word,
> and not hearers only,
> deceiving yourselves."
> **James 1:22**

D. Receptive heart

A receptive heart is one that allows itself to be taught, laying aside all self-reliance. It is one that knows the value of the Bible and never stops learning from it. Psalms 119:96 says:

> "I have seen the consummation of all perfection, but Your commandment is exceedingly broad."

Hold on to the Word and as you read it everyday, ask God to turn your heart into good soil, capable of receiving the seed and producing fruit -30, 60 and 100- fold.

II. HOW TO STUDY THE WORD

Everyone seeking God desires to hear His voice in a personal and direct way. It can be hard to believe that He is genuinely interested in us – that He loves and longs for us. John 14:31 says,

> "But that the world know that I love the Father, and as the Father, gave Me commandment, so I do. Arise, let us go from here."

When you are studying the Word, the place, atmosphere, and time play a fundamental role. That is why you need to keep these suggestions in mind:

A. Choose a proper place

Whenever possible, study at a desk as this will help you concentrate. Do not try studying on the bed when you are tired, because your good intentions will most likely turn into profound sleep.

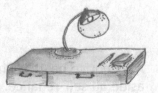

B. Buy a notebook and make it your devotional diary

This will allow you to write down all that God tells you and to be able to go over it again when needed.
It will help you evaluate your progress and retain what you have learned, because writing makes memorising easier.

C. Establish a study Pattern

According to your personal preference decide how you are going to interact with the Word each day. You can do this by determining the amount of time you are to spend or by establishing how many chapters you will study. Keep it the same every day.

D. Plan your daily devotions

Many people have the desire to study the Word and receive all they can, but because they do not have a specific study method their desires do not become reality.

For this reason we recommend Tim La Haye's method in his book, "How to Study the Bible for Yourself". This book explains the importance of applying the following four points to each passage:

Message from God for the day

This is what impacted you must from today's reading.

Promise of God for my life

A blessing God promises to give us. For example:
"And whatever we ask we receive from Him, because we keep His commandments and do those things that are pleasing in His sight." (1 John 3:22).
The promise is:"whatever we ask we receive from Him"

Commandment to obey

A promise generally has conditions for its fulfilment, These are the commandments for us to obey. In the above text the commandment would be, "because we keep His commandments and do those things that are pleasing in His sight."

Personal application

You need to change those things that God highlights to you. Establish a specific plan about how you are going to do this, and map out the steps that will accomplish it.

If your Bible study does not produce a change in you, you have not really studied. After studying there must come change in your life.

With this Bible study method you will be able to measure how much you advanced each day. Go back over your notes where necessary and study the Word again. Review what you have learned. I recommend that you start by reading the New Testament twice, before reading the Old Testament.

III. BENEFITS OF STUDYING THE WORD

A. It helps us conquer sin

When the Word of God is treasured in our heart we have a place to go when temptation comes knocking at our door. The Holy Spirit reminds us of a specific passage that will give us the victory. Jesus used the Word to overcome the devil the three times he came to tempt Him, by saying, "It is written...." Luke 4:4,8,10.  What is more, the Psalmist confirms this in **Psalm 119:11** when he says: "Your word I have hidden in my heart, That I might not sin against You!"

B. It prepares us to confront doctrinal errors

In Paul's letter to Titus, he explains it like this:

"Holding fast the faithful word as he has been taught, that he may be able, by sound doctrine, both to exhort and convict those who contradict." **Titus 1:9**

C. It helps us in spiritual warfare

The Bible is like a sword used to attack and defend.
With Bible verses we can confront the enemy and order him to
let go of our lives, finances, mind, and emotions. Ephesians 6:17
teaches:

> "And take the helmet of salvation, and the sword
> of the Spirit, which is the word of God"

D. It makes our prayers powerful

Jesus promises us that if the Word endures in us, we will
obtain the answers to all we ask.

> "If you abide in Me, and My words abide
> in you, you will ask what you desire,
> and it shall be done for you."
> **John 15:7**

E. It gives us full certainty of our salvation

When you first begin your walk with Christ one of Satan's
special weapons is to make you doubt your salvation. He brings
guilt into our lives to make us think that God has left us and
that we are no longer worthy of His forgiveness. That is why
the Lord assures us in 1John 5:13:

> "These things I have written to you who believe
> in the name of the Son of God, that you may know
> that you have eternal life, and that you may continue
> to believe in the name of the Son of God."

F. It gives us peace when we go thru affliction

In adverse circumstances, our sustaining force is the Word hidden in our hearts and the Biblical promises we have received from God. The Lord encouraged His disciples saying:

"These things I have spoken to you,
that in Me you may have peace.
In the world you will have tribulation;
but be of good cheer,
I have overcome the world."
John 16:33

G. It enables us to manifest our faith

Peter exhorts us to be ready to defend ourselves from those who would ridicule the gospel, and to be prepared to answer those who want to know more. It is important that we are able to explain our faith and confront every attack, whenever necessary.

"But sanctify the Lord God in your hearts, and always be ready to give a defense to everyone who asks you a reason for the hope that is in you, with meekness and fear…" **I Peter 3:15a**

H. It guides us through life's decisions

Drawing near to the Word will prepare you to face life with wisdom. God will instruct and give you direction concerning every decision in your life, family relationships, business, relationships, friendships, etc.

That is why the Psalmist affirms,

"Your word is a lamp to my feet
And a light to my path."
Psalms 119:105

I. It guarantees us a successful life

Joshua 1:8 explains, "You shall meditate in it day and night...
For then you will make your way prosperous, and then you will
have good success". You will carry the seal of success because
God will prosper you in everything you do.

After reading and meditating on the Word, always end your
time with prayer. Ask God to teach you how to apply what you
have learned during your Bible study. Seek His forgiveness for
the sins you comitted and ask Him to take control of every
area of your life. By doing this you will, without a doubt, find
success in everything you do.

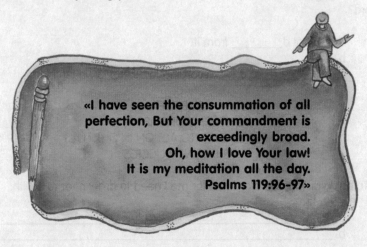

«I have seen the consummation of all
perfection, But Your commandment is
exceedingly broad.
Oh, how I love Your law!
It is my meditation all the day.
Psalms 119:96-97»

EXERCISE
THE WORD - THE FOUNTAIN OF LIFE

1. The Word is a fountain of Life and promises, but many times, we do not make use of it. Let us see what the Bible has to say about its importance.

Complete and memorize

a. Joshua 1:8
"This _____ of the _____ shall _____ _____ from your _____, but you shall _____ in it _____ and _____, that you may observe to _____ according to all that is written in it. For then you will make your _____ _____, and then you will have good _____."

b. Psalm 119:105 "Your _____ is a _____ to my feet and a _____ to my _____"

2. According to Joshua 1:8, what does the Lord want us to do with His Word?

    a. Do not d_____ from it
    b. M_____
    c. O_____ to d___ according to all that is written in it.

REMEMBER:
MEDITATING ON THE WORD
AND PUTTING IT INTO ACTION IN OUR LIVES
WILL BRING SUCCESS

3. To enjoy all that the Word has for me I need to draw near to it with:

    a. _____
    b. _____
    c. _____
    d. _____

4. Explain in your own words what it means to, "Have the right attitude"

_____

_____

_____

_____

5. Match the three words that follow with the statements below, knowing these three things will lead you to success in reading the Word.

__ Receptive heart   __ Meditate in it   __Obedience

a. A light in my life, that helps me discover the truths that impact my way of thinking and living in such a way that I desire to live its principles.

b. Turns me to action, and influences me, changing the way I live.

c. Humbly drawing near, understanding that every day there is something I need to learn, that will produce fruit in my life.

6. To study the Bible there are 4 important principles. What are they?

a. _____
b. _____
c. _____
d. _____

7. On the basis of what you have learned about having daily devotions, read **1 John 1:1** and find

a. The message of God _____

_____

b. Promise for my Life _____

_____

c. Commandment to obey _____

_____

d. Personal application _____

_____

_____

_____

READING THE BIBLE OFFERS MANY BENEFITS

8. What does Paul urge Titus to do in **Titus 1:9,** and why?

_____

_____

_____

9. According to **Ephesians 6:17,** What is the Bible for and how can I apply it?

_____

_____

_____

10. According to **John 15:7.** What should I do to have powerful prayers?

_____

_____

11. When we begin to walk with Christ, struggles arise to make us doubt our salvation. **I John 5:13** teaches us:

_____

_____

_____

_____

SEXUALITY

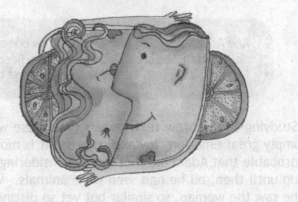

God wants everyone to be happy, He gave us the capacity to love and be loved. He established certain principles so that this can become a reality.

In their rush to find so-called «love», many people fall into illicit sexual relationships. Instead of being a blessing as God wills, it brings suffering wich steals their peace and dreams, leaving them with a broken heart.

God knows the consequences of sexual relationships outside marriage. He intends for you to understand His purpose so that you wait for His timing. He will bring you the ideal person, who will make you happy and together you will fulfil His purpose.

I. SEX, A CREATION OF GOD

God created man and placed him over all of creation. Nevertheless, out of all creation there was found no helper for Adam, "So Adam gave names to all cattle, to the birds of the air, and to every beast of the field. But for Adam there was not found a helper comparable to him.." Genesis 2:20, so God took a rib out of Man and created Woman.

> And Adam said: "This is now bone of my bones and flesh of my flesh; She shall be called Woman, Because she was taken out of Man." **Genesis 2:23**

Studying the Hebrew text reveals that these words imply great emotion, joy and surprise. It is most probable that Adam did feel these, considering that up until then, all he had seen were animals. When he saw the woman, so similar but yet so distinct, he said, "This is now bone of my bones And flesh of my flesh". He expressed the satisfaction he felt in knowing that she was the perfect complement to himself, and exactly what he needed.

And so, God celebrates the first wedding and unites them as a couple:

> "Therefore a man shall leave his father and mother and be joined to his wife, and they shall become one flesh."
> **Genesis 2:24**

The last part of the verse "*they shall become one flesh*" refers to a couple's intimate physical union, the sexual aspect. This is not shameful. On the contrary, it reflects the freedom of knowing each other without inhibitions.

> "And they were both naked,
> the man and his wife,
> and were not ashamed."
> **Genesis 2:25**

God looks at sex as something natural, and it pleases Him when it is experienced within His set parameters. He delights in love when it is honest and complete.

The Song of Solomon is an expression of the love between a man and wife, and a reflection of how intimate God wants marriage to be.

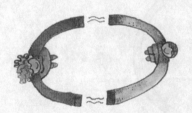

From the beginning, there has existed an affinity and mutual attraction between the two sexes. Relations among those of the same sex were not within God's plan. Otherwise, God would have given Adam another Adam instead of Eve. This wrong type of relationship is the fruit of forgetting God, and becoming wise in your own mind, giving yourself over to something that does not please the Lord.

> "Likewise also the men, leaving the natural use of the woman, burned in their lust for one another, men with men committing what is shameful, and receiving in themselves the penalty of their error which was due"
> **Romans 1:27**

These and other practices have emerged as a result of the fall of man. They have changed the parameters set down by God. They see sex as something purely for pleasure that should be experienced whenever you desire it, and with whoever you desire.

Some young people use sex to ensure that their partner will not leave them. In the end, these deceptions leave a profound feeling of loneliness, an inner emptiness, emotional conflicts, sexually transmitted diseases (including AIDS), unexpected pregnancies and forced marriages, among other things.

II. WHY WAIT AND HAVE SEX ONLY IN MARRIAGE?

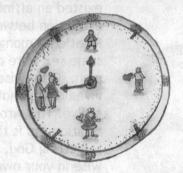

Though God Himself created sex for a good purpose, society has turned it into something degenerated, dirty, and distorted. Besides creating pressure through the means of communication (television, magazines, radio, telephone and Internet) society aims to trap people in illicit sex.

The strategies vary from nudity (programs containing sex scenes that excite the imagination) to suggestive and explicit advertising promoting premarital sex.

Premarital sex is portrayed as normal, and adultery is justified when the partner is no longer satisfying or attractive.

Many people let themselves become entangled in sinful sexual relationships without thinking of the following consequences:

    A. We sin against God
    B. We develop a guilt complex.
    C. Negative consequences arise in your life.
    D. Your testimony is ruined

A. We sin before God

When we give in to sexual relations outside of marriage we are sinning before God. The Word says in I Corinthians 6:13:

> "Foods for the stomach and the stomach for foods, but God will destroy both it and them. Now the body is not for sexual immorality but for the Lord, and the Lord for the body."

Every sin committed with the body is done against the Lord. This includes fornication, adultery and homosexuality.
1 Corinthians 6:9-10 tell us that no one who practice these sins will inherit eternal life.
From the instant we open our heart to the Lord, the Holy Spirit comes and abides in our lives. John 14:17 teaches us:

> "The Spirit of truth, whom the world cannot receive, because it neither sees Him nor knows Him; but you know Him, for He dwells with you and will be in you."

The fact that God is in us makes our body His temple, and if we practice sexual sins we dishonor the temple of the Holy Spirit.

When you fall into these shameful sins, Solomon's saying is fulfilled:

> "Stolen water is sweet, and bread eaten in secret is pleasant." But he does not know that the dead are there, that her guests are in the depths of hell."
>
> **Proverbs 9:17-18**

We sin against God and give in, when we believe what others say. "You don't know what you are missing!" or, "You're not cool!" Many have fallen trying to be in line with their friends, doing whatever they say. An active sexual life, outside of God's will, takes away your peace and creates a feeling of insecurity concerning God. It is accompanied by a terrible fear about what could happen as a result.

B. Guilt complex

Sin always appears to be pleasant and agreeable at first sight. What's more, many are trapped into believing nothing serious will happen as long as you know when to stop in time. That is how many get caught in the world of pornography and end up with serious guilt problems, slavery, and addictions to this kind of practice. Their self-esteem is very low and they are uncapable of sustaining a healthy emotional relationship with someone of the opposite sex.

I once read about the case of a man who found a pornographic magazine in the garbage. He picked it up, read it, and from that time on became addicted to pornography. Since he was timid it was easier for him to practice masturbation than to win a young lady and start a relationship with her. But because our sin nature can never be quenched, but always wants more, he started raping and murdering young ladies. He was finally caught, after having killed 17 of them.

This incident reflects how sin can enter our lives subtly, and if we allow it free rein, it can enslave us and lead us into terrible actions. Maybe you think, "I will never fall into such extremes!" or, "My heart will never allow me to become so evil!" But nevertheless, directly or indirectly many have practice, murder through abortion.

Abortion is as much murder as mass murder. Many justify their crime saying that the fetus is only a mass of cells, but the Psalmist remind us that:

> "Your eyes saw my substance, being yet unformed. And in Your book they all were written,The days fashioned for me, When as yet there were none of them." **Psalms139:16**

From the very moment of conception we become a human being created by God and have contact with the Creator who gave us life. You should neither practice nor become an accomplice to abortion. You do not have the right to decide over the life of a defenseless person. If you do, you will bring a curse over your life and Proverbs 14:12 will be fulfilled:

> "There is a way that seems right to a man, but its end is the way of death"

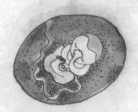

You will be filled by a deep agony when you realize that it was a life and there is now nothing you can do to change things. You will feel pain when you see a child and think how old yours would have been, and what he would be like if he were alive. Those who promote abortion will never tell you the consequences; but those who have experienced one know that they are real and painful.

Naturally, every sexual sin leaves a guilt complex, shame, and a web of deceit.

Many think they are no longer worthy of being loved. They become possessive in their relationships and end up begging for love, accepting physical, sexual, and emotional abuse. Some settle for being "the other person" in a relationship in order to keep it alive.

C. It brings negative consequences to your life

The painful, personal consequences of sexual sin can remain in effect for the rest of someone's life.
Many have fallen at a time when they least expected.
David, the king of Israel, is a clear example. One day, he was walking out on his palace terrace when he saw a very beautiful woman bathing. Not caring if she was married or not, he took her for himself and slept with her and she became pregnant.

Some might say that David simply obeyed his male impulses. I believe he fell because he gave his mind the freedom to wander and imagine whatever it pleased. What is more, his idleness also contributed to the sin. Instead of going to battle with his people, he was wasting his time at home.

Laziness is not a good influence, as it opens doors into our minds to things we should not think about. Once conceived in our mind these thoughts lead to sin and spiritual death.

This is what James teaches when he says:

> "But each one is tempted when he is drawn away by his own desires and enticed. Then, when desire has conceived, it gives birth to sin; and sin, when it is full-grown, brings forth death"
> **James 1:14-15**

David's adventure with Bathsheba, wife of Uriah, did not end there.

When David found out about Bathsheba's pregnancy, he sent for her husband and tried everything to make him sleep with her and cover up his sin. Uriah did not go to his house because his companions and nation were at war. Uriah's faithfulness caused David problems. He saw that the easiest way out would be to send a letter with Uriah to Joab, the general of his army. He orderer Uriah to be left alone in heavy battle, so to that he would be killed.

David's orders were carried out, and Uriah died on the frontline. Bathsheba was taken to the palace after having mourned her husband. David took her as his wife and she gave him a son.
A year passed. God waited for David to repent and confess his sin, but because he did not repent, his sin eventually caught up with him.

God sent Nathan to confront David about his sin. The prophet presented a story about a rich man, with many sheep who one day received a visitor. He went and slaughtered his poor neighbor's only lamb, one that had grown up with his children, eaten from his plate, and slept at his bosom.
When David heard the story, his anger was greatly aroused against that man and said: "...As the LORD lives, the man who has done this shall surely die! And he shall restore fourfold for the lamb, because he did this thing and because he had no pity." 2 Samuel 12:5-6

After David passed judgement, the prophet said, "*You are that man!*." Nathan, through a prophetic word, began to remind David how God called, prospered, and anointed him as king.

If all that had not been enough, the Lord was prepared to have given him more. God showed David the consequences of his sin. He told David that because he had killed Uriah the Hittite and took his wife, the sword would never depart from his house. His wives would be given to his neighbor, making what he did in private happen to him in public. Lastly, the son born to David and Bathseba would die. 2 Samuel 12:14

If David could have determined his own judgement he would have died, but God was merciful and gave him another opportunity. Yet, he lived with the pain of the consequences for the rest of his life.

The first thing David faced was finding out his son was to die. This caused pain and anguish in his heart. He stopped eating, bathing, and changing his clothes. He prostrated himself on the ground and humbled himself before God but the days passed and his son died. A short time after, God comforted him and gave him another son, King Solomon.

Later, he suffered seeing his children living the consequences of his past actions. David experienced sexual sin and violence in his own household. Amnon, one of his sons, raped his own sister, Tamar. Then Absalom, another one of his sons, killed Amnon out of vengeance for the affront and sexual abuse of his sister.

Absalom later rebelled, and tried to take David's kingdom. This caused David much anguish, "So David went up by the Ascent of the Mount of Olives, and wept as he went up; and he had his head covered and went barefoot." (2 Samuel 15:30)
While David fled, his son Absalom laid with his ten concubines in the sight of all Israel. (2 Samuel 16:22)

These things highlight a very painful truth in David's life because they were the consequences of his sin.
Proverbs 26:2 says

"So a curse without cause shall not alight"

Sin is not just a moment of weakness. It is a net that traps and leads to destruction of all who fall into it.

Today many young people experience the consequences of sexual sin. They suffer from venereal diseases such as herpes, syphilis, as well as AIDS. Some of these diseases are incurable and affect the person's children. It is terrible seeing children born infected with sicknesses that are a direct result of their parent's past sin.

After giving into pre-marital sex, some fall into sexual exploitation and become emotionally and physically affected. Others enter into the world of prostitution and having become one flesh with their clients, they receive the curses that their clients carry.

Hurt, pain, the bitterness from feeling used and abused, resentment and guilt complexes, are just some of the consequences of a promiscuous lifestyle.

III. HOW TO AVOID SINFUL SEXUAL RELATIONSHIPS?

There is nothing that helps us avoid falling into sin more than being aware of its consequences. However, you must take adequate measures to enable you to stand victorious when faced by sexual temptation.

A. Strengthen your relationship with God

A fall does not occur as a result of waking up one day and finding your carnal nature out of control. It starts with small indiscretions, things which open the door to temptation and later sin. This can come about in different ways with different people.

For men, their sight is what is most susceptible. The Lord says:

> "You have heard that it was said to those of old, You shall not commit adultery. But I say to you that whoever looks at a woman to lust for her has already committed adultery with her in his heart." **Matthew 5:27-28**

Sin begins when you look lustfully. It has been said that there is nothing wrong with the first look, it is the second look that is lust.

A woman is more sensitive to the things that she hears. If she allows compliments and flattery from people whom she knows are not right for her (someone already married, engaged, or leading an ungodly life), she is going to have problems. She may easily become entangled in a tormenting relationship that will produce negative results in her life.

The best way I can avoid a fall is by guarding my relationship with God, strengthening my prayer life, and depending on the Word of God.

A good start is to recognise our own past sins and weaknesses, and imitate David in obtaining God's forgiveness.

> "I acknowledged my sin to You, and my iniquity I have not hidden. I said, "I will confess my transgressions to the LORD, and You forgave the iniquity of my sin." **Psalms 32:5**

We need to confess every sin to God until we experience His forgiveness and the cleansing that Christ's blood brings. That is the only way to be freed from the curse sin brings.
The same must be done if you are going through temptation. If you seek God, He will give you a way out.

> "No temptation has overtaken you except such as is common to man; but God is faithful, who will not allow you to be tempted beyond what you are able, but with the temptation will also make the way of escape, that you may be able to bear it." **1 Corinthians 10: 13**

Determine to spend time praying and studying the Word each day. Do not allow one day to go by without talking to God and listening to His counsel. But, if in some circumstance you fail, ask God's forgiveness, confess your sin, and go on. This will guard your life from falling, and will bring profound strength that will allow you to prevail in all things.

B. Prepare yourself to face temptation

Temptations will come when you least expect them and in the most unusual ways. It is wise, therefore, to take precautions so we are not caught by surprise. Sexual insinuations and remarks are frequently used by those wanting us to give in to their flirting, sexual games, or even sex itself.

Phrases like: "If you really love me, then sleep with me!", "If you won't be with me, someone else will!", "If you are really a man, prove it to me!", "Everyone does it!", "If you ever want to see me again, you need to be more intimate with me!" are meant to pressure you into having sex without having an established commitment. You have to act with wisdom, and prepare yourself to confront these types of situations.

It's time to shine as children of God. Let us make a difference and show the world that we can be happy without sexual sin. We can be happy with our husband or wife, keeping our bodies for the person destined to be our lifelong mate. Let us produce families that reflect God's love and honour those things that please Him.

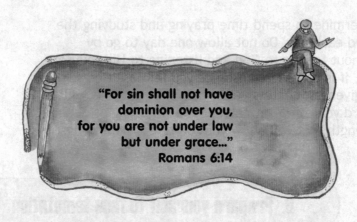

"For sin shall not have dominion over you, for you are not under law but under grace..."
Romans 6:14

EXERCISE
SEXUALITY

1. ¿Who celebrated the first marriage?
Genesis 2:24. _____

2. When it says in **Genesis 2:24**. _"...And they shall become one flesh,"_ what is it talking about?

_____
_____

3. What are the consequences of getting involved in illicit sexual relationships?

a. _____
b. _____
c. _____
d. _____

4. What does 1 Corinthians 6:13 teach about the use of the body?

_____

5. According to 1 Corinthians 6:9-10, what happens to those who practice sin?

_____
_____

6. According to **John 14:17,** who C_____ R _____ the Holy Spirit and why?

_____

7. Analyse **Proverbs 9:17-18** and answer the following questions in your own words.

    a. What is the "stolen water" and "bread eaten in secret?"

    _____

    b. Where can her "guests" be found?

    _____

8. Complete:
Sinful sexual life, _____
_____

9. Sin always appears to be:

    a. Pleasant   b. Shameful c. Disagreeable

10. Abortion is a form of murder. In what verse can we find that the fetus is a human being that has life?

    _____
    _____
    _____

           _____ (Biblical Reference)

REMEMBER:
SEXUAL SIN PRODUCES GUILT,
SHAME, AND LOW SELF-ESTEEM.

11. What things does the Prophet say will come about in David's life as a consequence of his sexual sin? **2 Samuel 12:5-6**

    a. _____
    b. _____
    c. _____
    d. _____

12. What should we do to stand victorious when sexual pressure comes?

a. _____

b. _____

REMEMBER:
A FALL IS NOT A RESULT OF YOUR FLESH GOING OUT OF
CONTROL, BUT RATHER SMALL INDISCRETIONS THAT OPEN
THE DOOR TO TEMPTATION AND LATER, SIN.

13. What would be a good start to avoid falling and also strengthening our relationship with God?

_____
_____

14. How can we be free from the curse that sexual sin brings?

_____

15. Is it possible to resist temptation? See. **1 Corinthians 10:13**

_____
_____
_____

THE CHURCH: GOD'S REFUGE

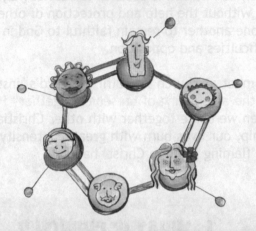

When we accept Jesus as our Lord and Savior, we become part of the family of God. It is His desire to offer us a refuge where He provides protection, care, and strength to live righteously with correction, direction, and discipline.

The family of God gives us new brothers and sisters; people who share our same goal (to follow Christ and be faithful to God). They will protect us from backsliding or turning back. We will backslide if we try living our Christianity independently and alone. It is wrong to believe we can survive as sons of God if we only listen to Christian radio or watch Christian videos on TV.

Just as a pieces of coal needs to be in contact with other coals in the fire in order to keep burning, we also need contact with other Christians to stay on the path that we have chosen. One coal, as hot as it may be, can't remain on fire if it stands alone. It must have heat and closeness from the other coals in the fire; left alone it would become cold. No believer, as firm as his decision for Christ may be, can be victorious without the help and protection of other believers. We need one another to remain faithful to God in the midst of trials, difficulties and opposition.

When we meet at church we fulfil the Lord's instruction "Not forsaking the assembling of ourselves together" Hebrews 10:25. When we come together with other Christians in prayer and worship, our lives burn with greater intensity, until we become a flaming torch in Christ' hands.

I. WHAT IS CHURCH ?

When believers meet together, we call that "Church". The church is a body made up by people in the entire world that have made the step of believing in Christ.

Because it is impossible to unite everyone in one place, the church has formed local fellowships all over the world.

The term «Church» literally means: "assembly of the called". The called are the believers and the church is not a building. It is the people that have believed in Christ and received Him into their heart.

From the moment you opened your heart to Christ, not only did you recieve a heavenly Father, but also new brothers and sisters. You became part of the family of God, the church.

The true church believes in the trinity, Jesus Christ as the Son of God, what He did for us on the cross and in the Bible as the fundamental basis for all doctrine. Church members manifest the presence of the Holy Spirit as in Matthew 7:20:

"Therefore by their fruits you will know them".

II. WHY DO WE NEED THE CHURCH?

The book of Hebrews emphasises that we must not neglect the assembling of ourselves together as «is the manner of some». During the Apostle Paul's days there were people with prejudices, fears and self-sufficiency who refused to do this.

The scholar Dr. Moffatt speaks of those that don't go to church because they fear the embarrassment of being ridiculed by friends and family. Some try to be secret disciples, but Moffatt says that this is impossible, because a "disciple" cannot by definition be "secret".

You either openly confess Jesus, or you are not a disciple at all! We need the church in order to be able to remain firm and faithful in our discipleship.

These are the reasons why we need to go to church:

A. It allows us to have fellowship with other believers

One of the names the Lord gives to His church is the "Body of Christ," with Himself as the "Head." Christ is the head of the Church." Ephesians 5:23

" Now we are the body of Christ, and members individually."
1 Corinthians 12:27

In this, God is showing us the value of each member and their importance in the body.In a body every part will need help at some time and must be prepared to give help.

By observing someone's reaction when they have been physically hurt we can understand how the body works.The hand will quickly move to help and comfort the injury, seeking to relief the pain. The same way, we in the body of Christ should always help one another by giving encouragement in times of trial.

It is difficult to remain stable and strong while with non-Christians. We will probably grow tired of swimming against the flow of opinion and end up yielding to sin. We need to carefully put King Solomon's advice into practice:

"Two are better than one; because they have a good reward for their labour. For if they fall, one will lift up his companion: But woe to him who is alone when he falls; For he has no one to help him up."
Ecclesiastes 4:9-10

In order to learn to have fellowship and develop strong friendships, it is necessary to get involved with church activities. Just attending church services is not enough! If fellowship only consisted of attending church services it would become very superficial. Real fellowship must take place in our natural enviroment, and in the course of normal everyday life.

We should find time to share together, go out to eat, talk on the phone, visit each other, participate in different church activities such as the Encounter weekends, post-Encounter meetings, School of Leaders and joining a ministry that allows us to develop our God-given talents.

B. We can receive counseling from mature Christians

The church gives room for every different ministry to develop. That is why we find people who are more spiritually mature than ourselves and with more experience in their walk with Christ. There are mature people that the pastors appoint to give us counseling when needed.

We should establish the principle of going to trustworthy people for help. If we detect some sin or bad habit that we cannot overcome, it is necessary to find help and receive counsel. That way we can overcome our problems.

Avoid counsel from those who do not know God because they lack divine wisdom, and may advise you to make decisions you will later regret:

> "The thoughts of the righteous are right: but the counsels of the wicked are deceitful."
> **Proverbs 12:5**

Many people who run to a non-Christian friend in a moment of difficulty, are now reaping the consequences of following that advice.For example, a certain young man had a misunderstanding with his wife, and later mentioned it to his non-Christian friend. The friend said, "Go, beat her, then leave for three days. When you return you will find her as meek as a lamb." He took his friend's advice. His wife never wanted to see him, or accept him back into the house again. She said she did not want a man like that at her side, because it would be a bad influence on her and the children.

C. We get the opportunity to serve

Just as every part of the body has its function, every believer in the body of Christ has a God-given gift or ability useful to minister to his brothers in the faith. For that reason Peter writes:

> " As each one has received a gift, minister it to one another, as good stewards of the manifold grace of God." **1 Peter 4:10**

These gifts vary from healing, to miracles, administration, and service, among others. 1Corinthians 12:28-30 gives us a long list of gifts, but the key is to use the gifts which the Holy Spirit has given to us. We can serve God's work in a responsible manner and with correct attitudes that reflect love.

When you go to church the goal must not only be to receive, but also to serve. Do whatever is within your power, and that way you will begin to discover your gifts. The Holy Spirit will encourage and help you in this.

Some gifts and abilities may seem insignificant in the eyes of man. They do not imply public recognition, or they are not visible to the eyes of many; but nothing we do is insignificant in the eyes of God. Everything we do for Him will be rewarded as the following story shows.

An elderly lady and a minister both passed away on the same day. He was a great preacher and she had been his intercessor. She had prayed for him constantly. When the minister got to heaven he thought to himself «I will receive a great reward for all my good preaching». Great was his surprise when the lady received more. When he asked why he was told, "The results you accomplished were the product of her prayers."

One of the characteristics of the apostolic church was its ability to serve. Waiting on tables and caring for the widows was very important to them they chose men of good standing, wise, and full of the Holy Spirit for the task. (Acts 6:2-3)

A good way to serve people is to share the good news of the love and forgiveness God offers them. We need to take the gospel to others and care for them, then we will see them transformed into the image of God. Serving others with the gospel will give you great satisfaction and it should become your way of life.

You can be useful in the church in many different ways. Share with others what you learned during the sermon, or give some personal testimony about how God has helped you. Just be willing to help out in whatever way no matter how small it may be.

D. It provides spiritual food

The main goal of a sound biblical church will be to prepare
believers for the work of the ministry:

> " For the equipping of the saints,
> for the work of the ministry,
> for the edifying of the body of Christ: "
> **Ephesians 4:12**

The teaching and ministry of the church must help
people to grow in the knowledge of Christ.
Only then will they be able to disciple others.
Another way the church ministers is by alowing the
move and ministry of the Holy Spirit. The church
must give the Holy Spirit freedom in worship and
prayer.

If there is anywhere you can grow spiritually and be edified it's
in church. The church is where you go from a spiritually
newborn baby into a mature Christian. The preaching of the
Word contributes to this growth.

2 Timothy 3:16 **says:**

> "All Scripture is given by the inspiration of God, and is profitable for doctrine, for reproof, for correction, for instruction in righteousness: "

When we teach and instruct through the ministry of the word, it brings conviction of sin, corrects and confronts what is wrong and shows how to live righteously.

Some people think they need to grow spiritually and become holy before qualifying to go to church; this is a mistake since the church's function is to mature you and give you direction.

Others go to church but think that if they sin they should no longer attend. The truth is that not even the greatest leaders have walked perfectly and without stumbling since the moment they gave their lives to the Lord.

They are in that position of honour because they have learned how to immediately confess their mistakes to God. They continued faithfully in the church, in spite of all the mistakes they have made. In church they heard the messages that brought about the changes in their lives. Even if you make a mistake and feel ashamed, confess your sin to God and do not miss church. The church will actually uphold and lift you up into new levels of victory.

Make the decision NOW to commit yourself to God and be faithful to Him and to the church family He has placed you in. Determine in your heart not to just occupy a seat at a church meeting, but rather give it the best of your time, commitment, companionship, and ministry.

If you do this, you will soon love your church, its vision and members. You will begin to feel that you have a large and beautiful family.

Come into a convenant with God TODAY, promise Him that whatever happens you will never abandon His church. You will be faithful at all times, even in trials, or when the world is pressuring you to separate you from God. If you do this, God's blessing will not be withheld from you, but it will touch your life and your family. You will see the hand of God in your life, helping and guiding you in all that you do.

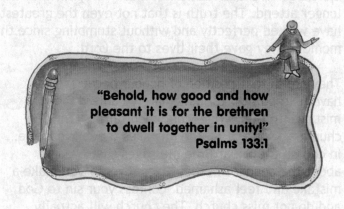

"Behold, how good and how pleasant it is for the brethren to dwell together in unity!"
Psalms 133:1

EXERCISE
THE CHURCH: GOD'S REFUGE

1. According to **Hebrews 10:25**, what should we NEVER stop doing?

2. Who is the church?

3. What is the difference between the church and the local church?

4.The word "church" literally means:

5. The true church believes in (tick correct answers):

      a. The Trinity
      b. Reincarnation
      c. Purgatory

6. The true church proclaims Jesus as

      a. A prophet
      b. A great teacher
      c. The Son of God
      d. All of the above

7. Dr. Moffatt says that people don't attend church because:

a. _____

b. _____

c. _____

8. Basing your answer on the last question, complete this phrase.
It is impossible to be secret disciples because:

"Either you live your life as a d_____ or s_____
does away with the d_____."

9. According to **1 Corinthians 12:27**, what is the church?

_____

10. To be able to remain firm in my Christian life (tick the correct answer):

a. It doesn't matter if my friends are unbelievers.
b. I only need God, no one else.
c. I need God and other believers to help me and uplift me.

11. According to **Ecclesiastes 4:9-10** why is it good to spend time and
become friends with other church members?

_____
_____
_____

REMEMBER:
IT IS NOT ENOUGH TO JUST ATTEND CHURCH SERVICES.
FELLOWSHIP OUTSIDE OF THE SERVICE IS IMPORTANT IN
ORDER TO GET TO KNOW THEM AND TO SHOW
THEM WHO WE REALLY ARE.

12. Write three activities you could become involved in wich will help you
meet other people.

a. _____

b. _____

c. _____

13. ¿Why is the advice of friends from church so good?
    According to **Proverbs 12:5**

    _____
    _____

14. What does the church provide you with and why?

    _____
    _____

A BALANCED LIFE

Our future is determined by how we manage our present life. It is essential that we establish our priorities. We must create the desire to grow like Jesus did, not just in one area, but in all areas of life. This will make us successful people. We will then have a positive influence on our environment -family, social life, work, and ministry.

> " And Jesus increased in wisdom and stature and in favour with God and men."
> **Luke 2:52**

This verse shows Jesus as our perfect example and shows the way by which we are to walk, following in His footsteps. It is important to see how Jesus did not conform to the world when faced with challenges and adversity. He did not become stagnant in life, but every day stirred Himself to do His best.

The word "growth" is a translation of the Greek word "prokopto". This means to drive forward, opening up the pathway. To progress as the Lord did in the four basic areas -intellectual, spiritual, physical and social.

I. INTELLECTUAL

The Word says: "And Jesus increased in wisdom..."

Wisdom refers to the intellectual aspect of our lives. It is the developing of the intellect; creating opportunities that make you smarter, more capable in your studies or work in a profession. You can become intelligent in every area of life. For example, at home you can set the goal to be a better son, father, mother, husband or wife.

God knows that only those who forsake negligence and laziness can achieve their goals successfully. They will mature and become better people. It is not enough to dream and desire something. To obtain it you have to act with diligence, consistency and discipline.

> "The soul of a lazy man desires, and has nothing: but the soul of the diligent shall be made rich."
> **Proverbs 13:4**

Lazy people always try to justify their behavior, but as time goes by they do not manage to progress.

People in that state become filled with frustration and feelings of incompetence. Proverbs 26:16 says, «The sluggard is wiser in his own conceit than seven men that can render a reason».

God does not want us to be frustrated and think that we are good for nothing. He is our the example of how to grow in wisdom in all areas. A good way to avoid being entrapped by lazines is to establish clear and concrete goals. This will help us give priority to what is truly important, and not get entangled with what appears to be urgent. Important things will lead us closer to our goals but urgent and unexpected things will lead us away.

We need to establish specific goals that will take us closer to our objectives. For example, deciding to read a book every month or week, taking basic courses to master computer skills, or to learn another language.
We need to take on the challenge to be the head and not the tail, to be the first and not the last in whatever we are involved in, whether this be at school, university, or in our career.

Consider your dreams and establish at least three goals and a specific time limit to achieve them in. That may be three months, six months, one year, or whatever length of time you feel is best. It is important that you define a time limit to your goal, otherwise they will just be good intentions.

II. PHYSICAL

"And Jesus grew in...stature." (Luke 2:52)

"Stature" refers to the physical aspect of our lives.
This encompasses our lifestyle, eating habits, nutrition and
recreation. These things influence our self image, as well as
how others see us.

A man of God by the name of Dick Iverson gave my husband
and I some advice. He recommended three practical things to
care for our physical condition: watch what you eat, play a
sport, and don't allow stress to dominate you.

I believe this man is right. It is smart to be balanced in
everything. That is why we should establish habits in our lives
that prolong our life and not shorten it because of bad health.
Some think it is not necessary to care for our bodies. They
abuse their bodies in youth and fall into excesses.
The consequences of this appears as they become older.

Excessive eating is when one consumes
an unbalanced measure of sweets, salt,
fizzy drinks and chocolates. We need to
establish new habits, checking to see if
what we are eating is healthy, and make
the necessary changes. You could start
by making small decisions to cut down
on chocolate, stop drinking fizzy drinks
for a week, or not putting so much salt
on your meals and so on.

Your rest should include activities like sport or exercise. They relief stress, as well as make you healthier. It is shocking to find young people whose only sport is spending all day in front of a TV. Their physical condition is so bad they cannot do the simplest exercise. They get sick if they try. Get involved in some sport, but don't fall into extremes. Many people turn their sport into their god and forget about the Lord.

Our appearance reflects who we are and the God whom we serve. Jesus set an example with His appearance. Though He was born in a poor stable, He excelled and dressed Himself with the high quality clothes of His time. He used tunics that were seamless, which were the best available. They were so good that the soldiers cast lots over one rather than divide it up. (John 19:23-24)

In our life we need to follow our Master and excel in the way we live, dress, and eat without making these things a god. We need to be a living testimony of what the Lord does for those who are faithful to Him.

III. SPIRITUAL

"And Jesus increased... in favour with God"
One of the things that brings great blessing is growth in the knowledge of God.

Matthew 6:33 affirms:

> "But seek first the Kingdom of God, and His righteousness;
> and all these things shall be added to you.."

This growth is manifested in constantly seeking God, knowing Him better and pleasing Him. Seeking God first brings rich blessings into the material, physical, emotional and spiritual aspects of life. The Apostle Peter advises us to establish spiritual goals, so that we always bear fruit. He encourages us to attain diligence, faith, virtue, knowledge, self control, patience, piety, brotherly affection and finally love. We must lift our spiritual life to new levels each day, so that our life can change in a positive way. That is how we fulfil 2 Peter 1:8,10:

> "For if these things are yours, and abound,
> you will be neither barren nor unfruitful in the
> knowledge of our Lord Jesus Christ."

Then Peter adds: "...for if you do these things you will never fall:"

If the search to become better moves into further levels, it is easy to forget the sacrifice of Christ on the cross, and the price He paid for our sins. That is why the best thing we can do to maintain spiritual growth is to hold steadfast to God. He will show us the areas in which we are giving ground to the enemy and show us how to be victorious. Then once again, we will be challenged to be better.

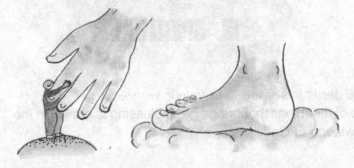

Jesus grew in favour by the power of God and the anoiting of the Holy Spirit. He was a success and multitudes of people were transformed, healed, freed and restored through His ministry.

This same Jesus now lives in us and as we grow in His knowledge and grace He will have the liberty to work through us making us a channel of blessing.

Our spiritual life will advance if we set goals and challenges. We should not be spectators in the work of God but become involved as active members. When we assume challenges we create a greater level of demand on the spiritual realm. For example, before teaching others, we must first prepare ourselves; we should review what we have learned and ask God for His empowerment.

The spiritual gifts flow when we create a need for them, God gives them to us in order to serve His people, not for us to boast about. As we get involved, in the work of the Lord He will lift us up and pour these gifts into our lives.

The apostle Paul tell us a great truth in 1 Corinthians 15:58

"Therefore, my beloved brethren, be stedfast, immovable, always abounding in the work of the Lord, knowing that your labour is not in vain in the Lord."

The text motivates us to be firm, to not be moved from our position we have in Christ. In others words to constantly do more than what we are asked to do, showing initiative and therefore continually improving.

Paul teaches that our work for
the Lord is not in vain.
Be assured of this and believe,
even if you currently don't
see the fruit. God alone knows
what we have achieved and
He will reward us. Set
specific spiritual goals so as to
avoid becoming stagnant.

Don't just attend the different church services, become an
integral part of the ministry. You can do this in the cells,
School of Leaders and encounters.

IV. SOCIAL

"And Jesus grew...in favour with... man."

To have a balanced life means not going to extremes and
giving each aspect of life its proper place. The Lord knows how
important people are that is why He spent time getting to
know them and meeting their individual needs. It gave Him
favour in front of the people. They wanted to share with Him,
listen to Him, be with Him and follow Him.

We should grow in our
relationship with those around us,
so as to be seen as people worth
following and imitating. What we
do, speaks louder than what we
say.

People should observe us and find
in us sincerity, love, human
warmth and an honest life. If
they see these things they will
open the door to their hearts and
desire to be a member of the
family of God.

When Samuel the prophet was young, he did not follow the bad example of those around him not even those living in the same house with him. He decided to become a man of integrity, and gained acceptance before God and the men of his time.

> "And the child Samuel grew in stature, and in favour both with the LORD, and men."
> **1 Samuel 2:26**

One of the places in wich we must guard our testimony is in our home. That will stregthen our relationships with our family members. Changes have a powerful effect at home because our family knows us and can totally notice our progress. We need to plan simple and achievable goals for ourselves.

For example, if we react with a bad temper when something goes wrong or we are offended, let's change. There must be real improvment in how we deal with others, our communication, our unity, our understanding and our fellowship.

We can not allow our goals in other areas of life to steal the time we spend with our loved ones. This can damage family relationships, create rifts and rob us of time for family fellowship. A young lady carried great sorrow in her heart. Each time her father had needed her for something she didn't have time. There was always something else to do. She didn't give him time, and when she finally wanted to, it was too late; her father died. She was left with great sadness and remorse because she could not go back and repair the damage. God wants us to be balanced in our family lives. He wants us to dedicate time and attention to our families, in order to win and nurture them for the Lord. Our testimony will also impact those who are close to our family.

Paul teaches Timothy:

> "Moreover he must have a good testimony among those who are outside, lest he fall into reproach and the snare of the devil."
> **1 Timothy 3:7**

A lifestyle of integrity can have a great impact on how positively people respond to us as integrity breeds confidence; They will know that we don't want to take advantage of them but want to influence their lives for good.

There is nothing worse than losing credibility with people, as it causes them to close the doors of their life to us. We must not compromise in our moral, ethical and biblical principles. Even the smallest compromise will stain our testimony.

Someone said: "People were made to be loved and things were made to be used". When we love people instead of using them we build solid relationships that reflect the integrity of our lives as believers.

If we follow Jesus' example, and grow intellectually, physically, spiritualy and socially, we will have a successful life.
Our life will be filled with personal satisfaction and blessings, not only for us, but also for our families and those around us.
Let us demonstrate to others with our example that they can have a better life when they follow the Lord.

Our testimony can give them an opportunity to turn to God and enjoy the blessing of living under His guidance.

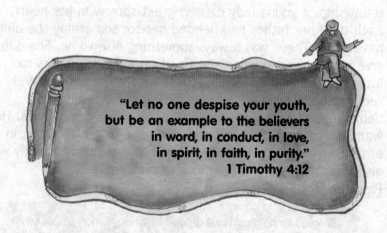

"Let no one despise your youth, but be an example to the believers in word, in conduct, in love, in spirit, in faith, in purity."
1 Timothy 4:12

EXERCISE
BALANCED LIFE

1. The Word teaches that Jesus was balanced in His growth. According to **Luke 2:52**, In what did He grow?

_____

_____

2. What does GROWTH mean?

_____

_____

3. What are the four aspects in which one should GROW?

_____

_____

_____

_____

4. What do we need to leave behind in order to improve ourselves intellectually and why? **Proverbs 13:4**

_____

_____

5. Given your previous answer, how can we avoid falling into the lazy man's trap?

_____

_____

6. What areas are part of our physical life?

_____

_____

7. In which area should I grow in order to bring more blessing and fulfilment into my life? **Matthew 6:33**

_____

8. Why is it important for us to establish spiritual goals in our spiritual life? **2 Peter 1:8-10**

_____
_____
_____
_____

9. Jesus grew in favour with God, which brought into His life:

The P_____, The G_____H_____
S_____ and a great M_____.

REMEMBER:
"JESUS NOW LIVES IN US AND IF WE GROW, IN HIS
KNOWLEDGE AND GRACE, HE WILL USE US TO BLESS OTHERS"

10. Our spiritual life will advance if we create _____ which brings us to a greater level of D_____.

Based on the previous:
MY _____ are:

_____
_____
_____
_____

11. When the gifts flow through us it is for what purpose?

_____
_____
_____
_____

12. According to **1 Samuel 2:26** what did Samuel the prophet decide in his youth?

_____

13. What should we focus on in order to improve our testimony in our own homes? Give some personal examples.

_____
_____
_____
_____
_____
_____

14. Why is integrity so fundamental for growth in the social area?
1 Timothy 3:7

_____
_____
_____

BALANCED GROWTH, NOT ONLY BRINGS SUCCESS AND
PERSONAL SATISFACTION BUT GREAT BLESSINGS
FOR US AND THOSE AROUND US.

BAPTISM A STEP OF OBEDIENCE

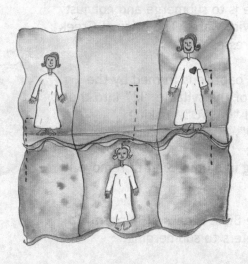

Before leaving this world people reflect on what is most important to them. Jesus did this when he explained the importance of being baptised before He ascended to the Father. It is recorded in Matthew 28:19:

> "Go therefore, and make disciples of all nations,
> baptising them in the name of the Father,
> and of the Son, and of the Holy Spirit."

The «Great Commission» states that every person we win to the Lord is to baptised. Jesus not only commanded baptism, but He Himself was baptised. This highlights the importance of baptism. It was the first step for Jesus Christ in His ministry. (Matthew 3:15)

There often arises a series of questions in regard to baptism:

I. WHAT IS BAPTISM

To baptise is to submerge and not just sprinkle with water. The original Greek word expresses this.

The word baptise is formed by the insertion of the syllable "IZ" into the root word "BAPTO", making "BAPTIZO". "Bapto" means "to submerge something in a liquid and to remove it again".

When the Bible speaks of baptism, it always refers to submerging.

II. TYPES OF WATER BAPTISM

Baptism of repentance

God used John the Baptist to preach the baptism of repentance as he prepared the way for the Lord. He called the people to repent of their sins so that they might be forgiven.
They were then baptised to seal their decision, and as a public testimony of their confession and change of lifestyle.

> John came baptising in the wilderness, and preaching a baptism
> of repentance for the remission of sins. And all the land of Judea,
> and those from Jerusalem, went out to him and were all
> baptised by him in the Jordan River, confessing their sins.
> **Mark 1: 4-5**

John the Baptist teaches us that we must prepare ourselves
for water baptism, and approach it with a genuine heart of
repentance. Your heart must be sincere, unlike the Pharisees
and Saducees that came to be baptised, in Matthew 3:7,8.
John challenged them to produce fruit in keeping with true
repentance. God does not want us to be baptised for
traditional or religious motives. Baptism is a living testimony
of the change in our lives, that we may live to please Him.

Baptism is obedience

Jesus was presented before God at the Temple, forty days
after birth (Luke 2:22). Nevertheless, it was not until He was
thirty years old that Jesus was baptised, having full
understanding of what He was doing.

> "Then Jesus came from Galilee to John at the Jordan , to be
> baptised by him. And John tried to prevent Him, saying,
> I need to be baptised by You, and you are coming to me?"
> But Jesus answered and said to him, «Permit it to be so now,
> for thus it is fitting for us to fulfil all righteousness.
> Then he allowed Him."
> **Matthew 3:13-15**

John the Baptist carried out a baptism that confirmed repentance for the forgiveness of sins. As Jesus was completely sinless, John did not want to baptise Him. He said that Jesus should baptise him instead. Jesus explained that it must be that way in order to fulfil all righteousness.

RESURRECTED TO A NEW LIFE

Righteousness is a translation of the Greek word "Dikaiosune" and means: "whatever has been appointed by God to be acknowledged and obeyed by man". Jesus fulfilled all the commands of God to give us this standing, including baptism.

Our baptism is a step of obedience. If Jesus had to do it to fulfil righteousness, how much more must we need to do it!

Matthew 3:15 in a modern translation says:
"John, Jesus answered, baptise me, because it is fitting for us to fulfil what God has commanded"

So why do we need to be baptised? The Scriptures teach that he who is baptised in water, is dying to the old way of living and being resurrected to a new life.

You can see this in Romans 6:4:

"Therefore we were buried with Him through baptism into death, that just as Christ was raised from the dead by the glory of the Father, even so we also should walk in newness of life."

III. PREPARING FOR BAPTISM

A. Believe

Everything we do in Christian life requires faith.
The Ethiopian Eunuch asked Philip: "What hinders me from being baptised? " Then Philip said, "If you believe with all your heart, you may." And he answered and said, "I believe that Jesus Christ is the Son of God." So commanded the chariot to stand still. And both Philip and the eunuch went down into the water, and he baptised him." (Acts 8:36-38).

The Bible has several examples of people getting baptised immediately after believing in Jesus: the three thousand converts in Acts 2:41, the jailer and his family from Philippi in Acts 16:33, and Crispus, the chief ruler of the synagogue of Corinth who with all those that believed with him was baptised in Acts 18:8. In all these cases baptism was preceded by faith in Christ and then practised at once..

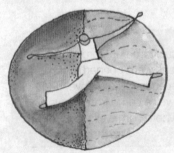

A basic characteristic in all these stories is that simple faith was all that preceded baptism. Therefore we should get baptised as soon as possible after we have placed our faith in Jesus.

B. Repent

Repentance must precede baptism. Repentance is a translation of the Greek word "Metanoeo" and means «change of mind or purpose». In the New Testament it always implies a «change for the better». Baptism demands repentance. It is to die to the desires of the flesh, bad habits, and to all those things that are wrong in the eyes of God, even if they seem right to us.

When Peter preached his first sermon, the people asked: "What must we do?"

Acts 2:38 tells us, "Then Peter said to them, "Repent, and let every one of you be baptised in the name of Jesus Christ for the remission of sins; and you shall receive the gift of the Holy Spirit."

Peter's answer shows us that if we want to be baptised, first we must repent. Remember that repentance is a change of mind and purpose, showing that it is Jesus who now governs our lives.

IV. BLESSINGS OF BAPTISM

Baptism has a special function in the spiritual realm. We are now resurrected to a new lifestyle that is pleasing to God. This opens us a path to the same blessings that Jesus received the moment He was baptised.

> "When He had been baptised, Jesus came up immediately from the water; and behold the heavens were opened to Him, and He saw the Spirit of God descending like a dove, and lighting upon Him. And suddenly a voice came from heaven saying, «This is my beloved Son, in whom I am well pleased."
> **Matthew 3:16,17**

Now when we have abandoned sin there is nothing that can come between us and the Lord, we have complete access to His presence. The heavens will open to us and we can conquer in the spiritual realm the things we want to conquer in the material realm. Isaiah 59:2 teaches us that only sin can separate us from God. If we overcome this obstacle nothing can separate us from the Lord.

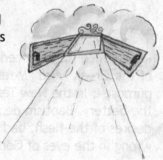

Jesus had the Holy Spirit descend upon Him. When we are baptised, it can help open our spiritual eyes to the Spirit of God. This enables us to receive God's guidance in our lives, and put our trust in His direction.

The Father affirmed His acceptance of Jesus with the words "This is my beloved Son". He was giving Jesus confirmation that in His human form He was the beloved Son of God. Then He expressed His pleasure in Him.

As we are baptised, God confirms to us that we are His children. We become His loved ones, those who are pleased to do His will. When we are baptised we receive all of these blessings from God, as well as publicly confessing our faith in Him.

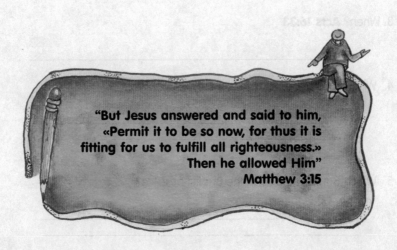

"But Jesus answered and said to him, «Permit it to be so now, for thus it is fitting for us to fulfill all righteousness.» Then he allowed Him"
Matthew 3:15

EXERCISE
BAPTISM - A STEP OF OBEDIENCE

1. What was Jesus' first public step in His ministry? **Matthew3:13-17**

   _____

2. What did the Phillipian jailer do after he heard the message? **Acts 16:29-33**

   _____

   _____

3. When? **Acts 16:33**

   _____

4. What types of baptisms are there?

   a._____
   b._____

5. Which Baptism did John the Baptist practice?

   _____

   _____

6. What requirements did this baptism have?

   a._____
   b._____

7. In **Matthew 3:7-8** , what did John the Baptist demand of the Saducees and Pharisees? See _____

_____

_____

REMEMBER: IN ORDER TO BE BAPTISED YOU MUST
DEMONSTRATE REAL CHANGES THAT SHOW TRUE REPENTANCE.

8. According to **Luke 2:22**, Jesus in His childhood was:

    a. _____

    b. _____

9. In **Matthew 3:13-15,** what type of baptism did Jesus practice?

_____

_____

10. What does "DIKAIOSUNE" mean?

_____

_____

11. Bearing in mind the previous question, why was Jesus baptised?

_____

_____

12. With which one of these two baptisms should you be baptised and why?

_____

_____

_____

_____

THINK ABOUT IT:
IF BAPTISM IN WATER IS NOT IMPORTANT,
WHY WAS THE LORD BAPTISED?

13. According to **Acts 10:47-48**, is it enough to have only the baptism of the Holy Spirit?

_____
_____

14. What do I need in order to be baptized? **Mark 16:16**

_____
_____

15. Baptism implies that I bury my past way of living **(Romans 6:4)** and only a _____ heart can distance itself from the sin that previously governed it.

16. According to **Acts 2:38** First I must

_____ and _____ of my sin, so that I may be _____ as public evidence of my actual position.

17. What blessings came upon Jesus when He was baptised?
Matthew 3:16-17

a. _____
b. _____
c. _____

WHEN WE ARE BAPTISED WE CONFIRM
EXTERNALLY THAT WE ARE THE BELOVED
CHILDREN OF GOD, AND HE TAKES
PLEASEURE IN US.

MUSIC AND ITS INFLUENCE ON OUR LIVES

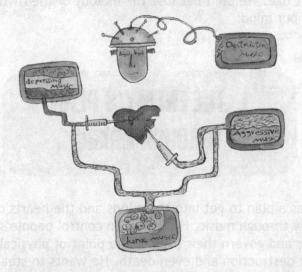

After an Encounter, we have a great desire to change our lifestyle, but sometimes we don't know how. During the encounter weekend we are shown the influence secular music has over our lives. For a lot of people, secular music is a major issue and we must know how to respond now that we are believers.

God created music but Satan distorted it. He used it to deceive many and steal the worship and praise that belongs to God. We can't ignore the fact that in each part of our body we have music. It is in our breath, our heartbeat and in each atom of our entire being. Having music within us is what makes us sensitive to different rhythms or melodies. It is natural - God made us that way.

We should not deprive ourselves from listening to music, but choose music that does not produce a negative effect within us. Music greatly influences our behavior. When we are stressed we can play soft and calm music that soothes the nerves and reduces anxiety.

Often we move our feet, fingers or head to the beat of rhythm that we are listening to or unconsciously we sing a song that we don't like. We do it because the melody or the rhythm got stuck in our mind.

I. THE ENEMY'S PLAN THROUGH MUSIC

Satan has a plan to get into the minds and the hearts of humanity through music. His goal is to control people's behavior and govern their lives to the point of physical and spiritual destruction and even death. He wants to steal everything that man loves: family, feelings, and friends. John 10:10 says:

> "The thief does not come except to steal, and to kill, and to destroy. I have come that they may have life, and that they may have it more abundantly."

122

II. SATAN'S PURPOSE THROUGH MUSIC

A. To steal God's praise and the abundant life of the new believer

Satan seeks to steal the honour and worship due to God. He influences people to sing and dance in a way that glorifies him. With the lyrics his music exalts the sins that God hates, like fornication, adultery, sexual pleasures unforgiveness and revenge. In this way Satan steals the souls of those that follow his music. He takes away the abundant life that Christ won for us on the cross.

When we sing songs like: "Take me one more time", we place words in our mind, words that awaken the flesh, its passions and sexual desires. These songs bring us to the point of yielding once more to the yoke of sin.

From my experience, I would say that those who can't renounce secular music still have the world in their heart.
Their Lord is not God, but secular music.

It is our responsibility to understand who we belong to. We must evaluate whether the songs that we sing, and the music we fill our minds with, is acceptable to Jesus. Would He enjoy it?

«He who is not with Me is against me, and he who does not gather with me scatters»
Luke 11:23

A young lady went on an Encounter shortly after becoming a Christian. There she saw the power of God. She turned away from her music and her unsaved boyfriend who would always call her while he was drunk. Sometime later she began to flirt with secular music again, especially with dance music which caused her to begin to backslide. It revived a desires to go to parties again, she got back with her old boyfriend and soon she was back into her old lifestyle of sin. Sadly she totally turned her back on the Lord, and the boyfriend left her with a fatherless child.

This young lady wasted her life and ruined the plan that God had for her. Her highest priorities were music and sex, whereas they should have been God.

B. To destroy the lives of its followers

Music has the power to destroy its listeners Mick Jagger, also known as the "Lucifer of rock", said: "WE ALWAYS WORK TO DIRECT THE WILL AND THOUGHTS OF THE PEOPLE, AND THE MAJORITY OF OTHER GROUPS DO THE SAME".

Through music at concerts, people are encouraged to do things which they would never do in other circumstances. Under the influence of music, some people strip off their clothes, revealing intimate parts of their body. They become involved in promiscuous sexual relationships.
They lose total control under the influence of drugs, giving themselves over to violence. This is often reported in the media after such bands have had a concert.

There is a famous saying: "The devil really pays those who serve him". The vandalism and evil doing that is encouraged by such music degrades the participants. They do evil, and it depresses them, releasing feelings of loneliness and defeat.

This has led many to the point of suicide. We should not allow ourselves to get involved in this type of Satanic music.

C. It spiritually and physically kills its followers

If you spend your time listening to music you will feel the desire to obey its message. Don't spend your time listening to sad, deppressive music - that only speaks about what could have been. If you listen to songs of discouragement or pain, you will end up depressed and defeated. It will make you drink to drown your sorrows, or make you consider the idea of suicide.

I knew a young 17-year-old high school student, who lived with his brothers and sisters. One day he began feeling extremely lonely and began to run around with the wrong crowd. He began to attend rock concerts where the young people would get high on drugs and fight each other. Some time later he shared with his family that he had made a decision about his life, and without any further explanation he went out the next day and shot himself.

One day he took a walk and shot himself.
The enemy's plan is to kill those that fall into his trap. He takes them to a place of torment where they think they can't get out. Many believers fall into his trap. They believe they are strong enough to resist temptation and run their own lives. They end up becoming slaves of their past: to liquor, to illicit sex, to violence and evil. They become sons of the devil, and lose the life that Christ won for them on the cross.

God wants to give us life and life in abundance. You will experience it if you set your mind on things which edify.
Seek music that gives you comfort and peace.
Listen to music that brings you closer to God and makes you a better person.

III. CHRISTIAN MUSIC GIVES YOU LIFE

A. It gives you peace and calms the spirit

Music touches our emotions and our will. What we listen to rules our thoughts, actions and attitudes.

While King Saul rebeled against God he lost His protection, and an evil spirit came and tormented him. Only when David played the harp would Saul feel peace, then the evil spirit would depart from him.

> "And so it was, whenever the spirit from God was upon Saul, that David would take a harp and play it with his hand. Then Saul would become refreshed and well, and the distressing spirit would depart from him."
> **1 Samuel 16:23**

Music exercises power over the people that listen to it. That power can be good or bad, depending on the type of music that you choose. When we listen to Christian music we release the presence of God in our lives and in our homes. We cast out all spirits that seek to oppress us. The people who visit us will feel the peace and the presence of the Lord. Like Saul we will feel free and peaceful through anointed music. (1 Samuel 16:23)

B. It's a useful tool for winning souls

Christians make excellent music. It is pleasant to the ear and has a positive influence on the listener. To share our music with non-Christians is a great testimony if it is of a high standard . Our music is an alternative for those who don't know Jesus. It breaks down the mind-set that church is nothing more than boring or mediocre.

In 1996 the Christian rock band «Petra» gave a concert in the Sports Palace of Bogota. The objective was to evangelise and show the world an alternative to secular music. Those who attended were impacted greatly. The media was impacted also and spoke higly of the musical quality of the band, and the spirit in which they performed. Then the people left having received the message of the gospel.

Music is one of the best instruments for soul winning. In that concert more than eight hundred people received the Lord as their saviour.

C. It Edifies

All Christian music has a positive and encouraging message, no matter what style it is; plus the melodies bring you closer to God. It creates an appropriate environment for prayer. You can enjoy a wide range of Christian music: rock, salsa, soul, disco, techno, country, metal and so on.

The Apostle Paul affirms in 1 Corinthians 6:12:

> "All things are lawful for me, but all things are not helpful. All things are lawful for me, but I will not be brought under the power of any."

It's not about rules and regulations, but knowing how to select music which is edifying. Christian music makes you feel better as a person. It gives you confidence, and strength in times of anguish and it brings you closer to God with its melodies and lyrics.

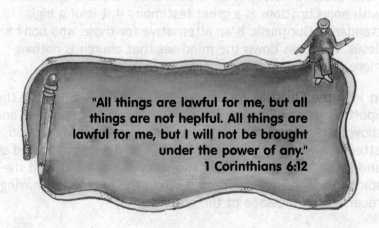

"All things are lawful for me, but all things are not heplful. All things are lawful for me, but I will not be brought under the power of any."
1 Corinthians 6:12

IV. HOW TO DEAL WITH MUSIC NOW THAT I AM A CHRISTIAN

1. Do not compromise with secular music. You could easily be trapped by your old habits.

2. Determined to think about something else when you have to listen to secular music in a public place.

3. Don't listen to music that revives memories or past negative experiences because this could take you back to your old ways and habits.

4. Maintain transparency in everything. Be conscious that the Holy Spirit sees everything and is there to help you.

5. When you don't want to contaminate your heart, speak in tongues, memorise Bible verses and think about the good things that God has given you.

6. Destroy the music that enslaved you in the past. Believe that God is able to give us much more than we can ask or understand.
(Deuteronomy 7:26 and Acts 19:19)

7. Buy good Christian music according to your personal taste and listen to Christian radio stations.

EXERCISE

MUSIC AND ITS INFLUENCE IN OUR LIVES

1. Music is an instrument created by _____ and distorted by
_____

2. Why are we attracted to different rhythms and melodies?

_____

_____

3. As for music we should: (Choose the best answer(s))

a. Throw away everything because it is from the devil
b. Listen to all types of music because my body has music within it
c. Be selective in our listening
d. Wean myself off the music that is not good for me little by little

MUSIC CONDITIONS OUR BEHAVIOUR:
IT INCITES US, OR IT CALMS US.

4. Because Satan knows the Power of music he uses it to: **John 10:10**

a._____

b._____

c._____

5. What does Satan steal through music?

_____

_____

6. According to **Luke 11:23** what happens to people who still have secular music in their heart?

_____

_____

7. How does Satan use music to destroy?

_____

_____

_____

_____

8. How does Christian music affect our life?

_____

_____

9. Christian music is an effective instrument for:

_____

_____

10. **1 Corinthians 6:12** in first person.

_____

_____

_____

_____

HOW TO KNOW
THE WILL OF GOD

To know God is a great blessing, but how much He can work in our lives depends, many times, on the decisions we make.

It is a great advantage that we have the Holy Spirit and can depend on His direction and guidance.

God doesn't make mistakes. He knows what is best for us and is willing to give it to us.

Proverbs advises us:

> "Trust in the LORD with all your heart, and lean not on your own understanding; In all your ways acknowledge Him, and He shall direct your paths."
>
> **Proverbs 3: 5-6**

Wrong decisions are a result of doing things our way and not taking God's advice into account. This can happen because we don't realise that He is interested in the small things, or we don't believe that the Bible has the answer to our needs.

I. BENEFITS OF DOING THE WILL OF GOD

If we want to have wisdom and assure a successful future, we need to stop making hasty decisions that we may later regret. That is why we need to consult with God and seek His guidance. He never makes mistakes and chooses the best for us. He loves us and His thoughts are good and not evil. He wants to give us the things we dream of and the happiness we long for.

Jeremiah describes it in the following manner:

> "For I know the thoughts that I think toward you, says the LORD, thoughts of peace, and not of evil, to give you a fututre and a hope."
> **Jeremiah 29:11**

To believe God and trust in Him is the best way to secure our future. God is like a pilot that sees the whole picture. He Knows the things that benefit us and the things that would hinder us. Acting in wisdom is seeking His advice and obeying Him.

Romans 12:2 says:

> "And do not be conformed to this world, but be transformed by the renewing of your mind, that you may prove what is that good and acceptable, and perfect will of God."

This verse expresses three truths about the will of God -It is good, acceptable (pleasing) and perfect.

The word "good" is a translation of the Greek word "agathos" which means, "something that is good in character with beneficial results". It is good because it comes from God whose nature is kind. He desires to give us the best, so that we can fully enjoy the life that Christ won for us on the cross.

Pleasing (acceptable) means that it is satisfying for us in every aspect. God knows what we like and according to this He chooses the best for us. We should not be afraid to trust in God. He knows us better than we know ourselves and gives us the best.

Some people fear submitting their emotions to God. They think that God will give them the opposite of what they desire and that He ignores their needs.

Some men who don't like talkative women think that the Lord will give them a wife who is like a parrot. Women who do not like unemotional and cold men are almost certain that God will give them one who never expresses his feelings. But God is not cruel.

"Perfect" comes from the Grek word «Teleios», which means capacitating us to realize the true end or purpose of our existence. The Beacon Commentary says that "Telion" means "the experience of fullness, to be complete". We can understand that by doing the will of God we develop ourselves to maximum potential, and understand our future existence under His will.

II. HOW TO KNOW THE WILL OF GOD

To understand the perfect will of God we have to complete several steps that establish His purpose in our lives:

A. Die to my own will in order to obey whatever God says

The Lord has given us the gift of will power, the ability to choose. When we lived without Christ we made decisions ignorant of His will. Now, it is necessary for us to die to our feelings, to what we think, to our old way of doing things, and submit to His will. We must not try to manipulate God through prayer. "Lord, let your will be done, but please let your will be what I want."

When it comes to romance, I have always believed that we should pray for our ideal spouse. We should give the specific characteristics we desire; that he or she is sweet, tender, loving, expressive etc. We should also maintain a neutral position. We can't pray for a particular person or name someone that we think should be our spouse. Many have wrongfully invested their time in this, but God does not yield to our every whim, no matter how much we insist.

Before I got married, I heard that a certain woman from the church had prayed for a whole year for my fiance.
She was convinced that due to her constant persistence, God would put an end to our relationship and César would be her husband. It didn't work and we got married. Disillusioned, she went to another church.

God doesn't make mistakes. We would live wisely if instead of clinging to what we want we would die to ourselves and wait on God; He knows what is best for us.

The Lord says in Isaiah:

> "For my thoughts are not your thoughts, nor are your ways My ways," says the Lord. "For as the heavens are higher than the earth, so are My ways higher than your ways, and My thoughts than your thoughts."
> **Isaiah 55: 8-9**

We need to die to doing things our way, and submit ourselves to the will of God. He will give us what is best for us, even though it may not necessarily be what we wanted in the first place. We must trust His will and understand that His decisions are better than ours. He doesn't make mistakes, and will always have the best for our lives.

B. Search for God's counsel through His Word

> "Thy word is a lamp to my feet, and a light to my path."
> **Psalm 119:105**

The Bible has the answer for each and every one of our needs -financial, emotional, studies, and family needs.
We need to come to the Word to seek what it says about our requests. If what we ask for is in accordance with the will of God, it will be confirmed through the Word.
If you don't know how to recognise God's direction ask Him for wisdom, and He will give it to you abundantly without reproach.

> "If any of you lacks wisdom, let him ask of God, who gives to all liberally, and without reproach; and it will be given to him."
> **James 1:5**

Look for biblical verses according to your needs, and God will speak to you.
The Word has that special ability to penetrate the most intimate parts of man, discerning all thoughts and intentions of the heart. (Hebrews 4:12)

A few years ago, when we were unable to buy an apartment, I began to search the Word relentlessly. God gave me Psalm 127:1,2 "Unless the LORD build the house, they labour in vain who build it. Unless the LORD guards the city, the watchman stays awake in vain. It is vain for you to rise up early, to sit up late, to eat the bread of sorrows. For so He gives His beloved sleep."
Then I understood that I was not going to find a place to live by wandering from one place to another. He told me that everything I did would be in vain if He did not grant it to me. He told me to wait. He said that He would give it to me and I wouldn't have to look for it. A few months passed, and the Lord performed a miracle. He gave us an apartment that was exactly how we had asked in prayer. I did not have to go out to look for it. He just sent the person that took us to the right place, and did the rest.

C. God gives us the desire to do His will

> "For it is God who works in you both to will and to do for His good pleasure."
> **Philippians 2:13**

One of the signs that confirms that we are moving according to the purpose of God is that He will incline our heart to His desire because He loves us, as the Word says He does it "of His good pleasure".

Pastor Yonggi Cho says, that it is fundamental that we submit the desires of our heart to the trials of time. If they come from Satan or from the flesh, they will fade away, but if they are from God they will remain. Remember that the desires of God are always according to the Word.

This is how Psalm 33:11 confirms it:

> "The counsel of the LORD stands forever, the plans of His heart to all generations."

D. God places peace in the heart so as to confirm His will.

> " And the peace of God, which surpasses all understanding, will guard your hearts and minds through Christ Jesus."
> **Philippians 4:7**

One of the most trustworthy signs for recognising the will of God is that you have peace in your heart. It is an internal peace regarding the decision that we are about to make, a peace that surpasses our understanding. It is God who gives this peace. He removes doubt and uncertainty and brings complete security and assurance.

This assurance cannot be based on good reasoning. We can demonstrate an apparent security, but we can't silence that internal voice which says "No, don't do it, that's not how it goes". That's the voice of God telling us that the way we are thinking is not according to His will.

In this case, you must seek the Lord in prayer, be honest with Him, tell Him your most secret thoughts. Ask Him to put a stop to your plans, if they are not His will. But if it is His will then affirm our thoughts. Some Christians pray for their relationship with unbelievers. They don't want to give their relationship up but they pray that God would do His will. When God speaks to the heart and to the deepest part of their being, they will begin to doubt, and they will not have peace about their future with that person.

Then, knowing that God doesn't approve of the relationship, they still don't obey Him. They always have an excuse, justifying it time after time. They always give the unbeliever one last opportunity. When that opportunity is missed, they still don't break the tie. Without realising that they are squandering their life in an unfruitful relationship. At some point they will realise the mistake they have made, but by then it is far too late. Their pain is always the result of not seeking God. King Solomon expressed it this way:

> "Commit your works to the LORD, and your thoughts will be established."
> **Proverbs 16:3**

The Holy Spirit works on the deepest part of your heart. He places feelings of confirmation or disapproval. He gives you a deep conviction of His perfect will, and a sense of peace that is beyond your understanding.

E. Circumstances will favour us

When we are moving in God's way, circumstances will turn in our favour. When we are not, we will see them turning against us through adversities and difficulties.

The Bible tells the story of Balaam who acted against the will of God. He wanted to go and curse Israel, he consulted God but God answered saying:

> "You shall not go with them; you shall not curse the people, for they are blessed." **Numbers 22:12**

Nevertheless, Balaam' selfishness was greater than his obedience, and he ended up going to that place to curse them.

God used a mule to stop him. The mule refused to move and even spoke. Then when he tried to curse them three times, God changed his curses into blessings.

We need to recognise when God is not involved in what we are doing. If we see that something always goes wrong, and things don't go as planned, the smartest thing to do is to not fight against the current. Instead, step back from this situation and wait on God. He will have something better for you.

I am convinced that if you follow these five steps you will secure your future. You will have the direction of the wisest Being in the universe. He sees everything and knows and wants the best for your life in every aspect.

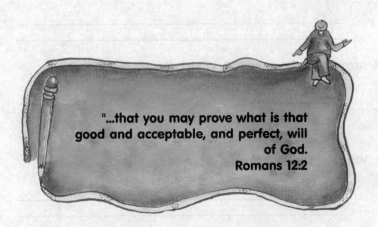

"...that you may prove what is that good and acceptable, and perfect, will of God.
Romans 12:2

EXERCISE
HOW TO KNOW THE WILL OF GOD

1. According to **Jeremiah 29:11** , Why can we rest on the fact that the will of God will give us the happiness that we yearn for?

_____
_____

2. According to **Romans 12:2,** What is the will of God like?

a. _____
b. _____
c. _____

3. What does it mean that the will of God is perfect?

_____
_____

4. What is the first step in knowing the will of God?

_____
_____

5. What does the Lord use to guide us in His will? **Psalm 119:105**

_____
_____

6. To what test is it necessary for us to submit our desires? Why? **Psalm 33:11**

_____

_____

7. What does God put in us to confirm His will?

_____

_____

REMEMBER:
"COMMIT YOUR WORKS TO THE LORD, AND YOUR THOUGHTS
WILL BE ESTABLISHED."

8. The Bible tells the story of Balaam, who moved against the will of God:
What can we learn from this story?

_____

_____

_____

_____

"TRUST IN THE LORD WITH ALL YOUR
HEART, AND LEAN NOT ON YOUR
OWN UNDERSTANDING."

BIBLIOGRAPHY

William Barclay, New Testament Commentary, Volume 13, Editorial CLIE, 1994. P.142

William Bright, The Ten Basic levels of Christian Development, Editorial Vida, Third reprint, 1998

Cesar Castellanos, Encounter. First Edition 1996

Billy Graham, The Holy Spirit. Baptist House Publications, Third edition 1986. P.89.

William M. Greathouse, BEACON Bible Commentary. Tome 8, Nazarene House of Publications, First Revised Edition, 1991.

Today's Bible, International Bible Society, 1979. New Testament. P.3.

Tim LaHaye, How to study the Bible for yourself, Bethany Editorial, 1977. P.29-34.

Josh McDowell, How to prepare your children to say NO to sexual pressure. Editorial UNILIT. First Edition 1990.

Derek Prince, The Christian Manual Filled with the Holy Spirit, Charisma Editorial Group, 1995. P.173.

Kenneth N. Taylor, The next steps for new believers, Editorial UNLIT, 1992

Richard Taylor, BEACON Bible Commentary, Volume 10, Nazarene House of Publications, second edition 1992 P. 383

E.W. Vine dictionary, exposition on words from the new testament. Volume 1. Graphic workshop print from Horeb M.C.E. copy 1984 by CLIE

Paul Yonggi Cho, Editorial Vida, fourth reprint, 1986. P.89.